CW00344358

1 MONTH OF
FREE
READING

at

www.ForgottenBooks.com

By purchasing this book you are eligible for one month membership to ForgottenBooks.com, giving you unlimited access to our entire collection of over 1,000,000 titles via our web site and mobile apps.

To claim your free month visit:

www.forgottenbooks.com/free916848

ISBN 978-0-266-96711-8
PIBN 10916848

LEWIS EVANS HIS MAPS

OF 1749 AND 1755

AND THEIR DERIVATIVES

OF THE

MIDDLE BRITISH COLONIES
IN AMERICA
A COMPARATIVE ACCOUNT OF
EIGHTEEN DIFFERENT EDITIONS PUBLISHED
BETWEEN 1755 AND 1814
TOGETHER WITH SOME NOTES DESCRIPTIVE OF
HIS EARLIER MAP OF 1749
THE WHOLE ILLUSTRATED BY TWENTY-FOUR FACSIMILES
OF TITLES AND MAPS

THIRD EDITION
(BEING A REISSUE OF THE SECOND)
WITH SOME ADDITIONAL NOTES ON
A SECOND EDITION OF THE MAP
OF 1749 PUBLISHED IN 1752
RECENTLY BROUGHT TO LIGHT
(WITH A FACSIMILE OF THE SAME)

By HENRY N. STEVENS, M.A., F.R.G.S.
• • •

LONDON

HENRY STEVENS, SON AND STILES
39 GREAT RUSSELL STREET, OVER AGAINST THE SOUTH-WEST
CORNER OF THE BRITISH MUSEUM
1924

PRINTED IN GREAT BRITAIN.
CHISWICK PRESS: CHARLES WHITTINGHAM AND GRIGGS (PRINTERS), LTD.
TOOKS COURT, CHANCERY LANE, LONDON.

LEWIS EVANS HIS MAP

OF 1752

IN the second edition of my Essay on *Lewis Evans his Map of the Middle British Colonies in America* (1755), published in 1920, some account was given of his very rare earlier Map of 1749. As the present Notes are intended to be merely additional, it is not necessary to go over the original ground again. Suffice it to say that in the account of that map a quotation was given from Evans' *Analysis*[1] in which he makes reference to a second edition which evidently must have been published in the interim between 1749 and 1755.

Diligent search failed to locate any copy of such a map, or in fact any other reference to it. A facsimile of the map of 1749 was given and a request made that " if anyone possesses or knows the where-" abouts of a copy of the Map of 1749 of a different impression to the " one here reproduced, he will greatly oblige by communicating " particulars."

No response was received and success was almost despaired of, when quite by chance a copy turned up in an old volume of miscellaneous maps which I was fortunate enough to acquire during my visit to the United States in the summer of last year.

As suspected, the Map turns out to be a re-issue of the plate of 1749 with sundry alterations and corrections. A comparison of the facsimile here given, with the one of the original issue of 1749

---

[1] The pamphlet he wrote in 1755 to accompany his *General Map of the Middle British Colonies in America* published the same year.

appended to the second edition of my Essay on Evans will prove both interesting and instructive.

No alteration has been made in the Title heading, as may be seen from the reduced facsimile given as a head-piece on the previous page. But an addition has been made to the original imprint in the top left corner immediately to the left of the title cartouche. The complete imprint now reads, *Published by Lewis Evans | March 25 1749 according to | Act of Parliament. | The Second Edition July* 1752. | It is to be supposed that the engraver's name, *L. Hebert sculp^t*, which in the edition of 1749 appears just below the bottom border line in the extreme right-hand corner, still remained on the plate. But as the copy of the Map under notice is trimmed close to the border line, the engraver's name has presumably been cut off.

There are numerous and important alterations and additions in various parts of the plate. Firstly there are the attempted corrections in the place-names on the west side of Delaware Bay, to which Evans specially refers on page 3 of his *Analysis* :

> " In the firſt Impreſſion of my former Map I committed ſome Miſtakes in
> "the Names of Places, near the Entrance of Delaware Bay on the Weſt Side,
> "and in my Attempt to rectify them, in the ſecond Edition, did but add to the
> " Confuſion " etc., etc.

Then there are important alterations in the boundary lines of Pennsylvania. The old northern boundary shown by a dotted line at 42° in the Map of 1749, lettered " *The Bounds of Penſilvania by Patent* " still remains, but a fresh dotted line has been added at about 42° 44', with a new lettering, " *The Royal Patent granting Mr Penn 3 Deg. of* " *Lat. & a Decree in | Chancery determining his ſouthern Limits will* "*probably extend | the Northern Bounds of Penſilvania to this Latitude.*"

The southern boundary of Pennsylvania, which in the Map of 1749 was shown by a dotted line at 39° 44', is now emphasized with an additional black line. Under the old lettering, " *Temporary Limits run* "*in* 1739 " *etc.*, there is now an additional three line inscription " *N B* " *The black Line ſhews the true Limits, according to a De- | cree in* " *Chancery, May* 15. 1750. | " Another new dotted line joins the black line at right angles and shows the boundaries of the three Delaware Counties, Newcastle, Kent, and Sussex.

In the top left-hand corner the outline of the southern shore of Lake Ontario is now extended west from Oswego (right through the engraved text of the long descriptive note) until cut off by the left-hand border line.

A new dotted line extends from near the junction of the West and East branches of the Susquehanna River eastward to Viskill on the East Branch of the Delaware River. This line is lettered " *Releafed by the Indian Kuttoongaliacs from the Kittatinni Ms. to this Line Aug.* 22. 1749."

Several new Counties have been added in southern Pennsylvania, such as Cumberland, York, Berks, and Northampton, with their boundaries shown by dotted lines. The positions and bounds of certain other Counties such as Lancaster, Bucks, and Philadelphia, have been considerably altered. In some places the erasures of the original letterings are faintly discernible. Numerous additional place-names have also been inserted, mostly in the new counties of southern Pennsylvania.

This Map is a further testimony to the conscientious and pains-taking efforts of Evans to bring his work up to date. When one considers the enormous extent of the Country covered by this Map, and the difficulty of making careful surveys in wooded and mountainous districts very largely unexplored and unsettled, it is marvellous that so high a standard of general accuracy should have been attained. In his *Analysis* of 1755, page 3, Evans explains the principal errors which had crept into this Map and how they had been rectified in his new *General Map* of *The Middle British Colonies* published that same year. The Map of 1755 for a long period was the principal prototype for the cartography of British North America, and in my Essay on Evans (2nd Edition) no less than seventeen direct derivatives from it, issued at intervals during the next fifty years or so, are tabulated and described. Moreover its indirect influence can be traced in almost every other map of North America made down to the end of the century.

At the time of his death in 1756 Evans had in contemplation the issue of a series of separate Maps of the several Colonies on a larger scale, in which he tells us he would have been enabled to include certain sectional and physical features which he had been compelled to omit from his small scale *General Map of the Middle British Colonies* for want of space. It is greatly to be deplored that his untimely death at the age of fifty-six should have prevented the completion of that admirable project. A series of large scale separate maps of the various Colonies made at that early date would have proved of inestimable historical value at the present day.

In conclusion it need scarcely be said that if any reader can communicate any additional information respecting Lewis Evans and his work, I shall be extremely grateful.

HENRY N. STEVENS.

March 1924.

At the time of his death in 1756 Evans had in contemplation the issue of a series of separate Maps of the several Colonies on a larger scale, in which he tells us he would have been enabled to include certain sectional and physical features which he had been compelled to omit from his small scale *General Map of the Middle British Colonies* for want of space. It is greatly to be deplored that his untimely death at the age of fifty-six should have prevented the completion of that admirable project. A series of large scale separate maps of the various Colonies made at that early date would have proved of inestimable historical value at the present day.

In conclusion it need scarcely be said that if any reader can communicate any additional information respecting Lewis Evans and his work, I shall be extremely grateful.

HENRY N. STEVENS.

March 1924.

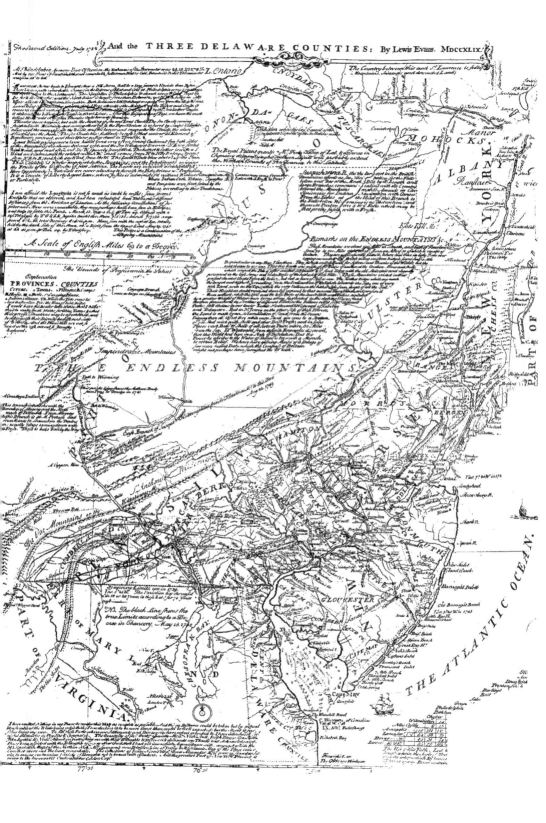

LEWIS EVANS
HIS MAPS OF
1749 & 1755

HIS MAP

OF THE

MIDDLE BRITISH COLONIES

IN AMERICA

A COMPARATIVE ACCOUNT OF
EIGHTEEN DIFFERENT EDITIONS PUBLISHED
BETWEEN 1755 AND 1814

SECOND EDITION
WITH NUMEROUS CORRECTIONS AND ADDITIONS
INCLUDING SOME ACCOUNT OF HIS EARLIER

MAP OF 1749

THE WHOLE ILLUSTRATED BY TWENTY-FOUR
FACSIMILES OF TITLES
AND MAPS

BY HENRY N. STEVENS F.R.G.S.

LONDON
HENRY STEVENS, SON, AND STILES
39 GREAT RUSSELL STREET
OVER AGAINST THE SOUTH-WEST CORNER OF
THE BRITISH MUSEUM
1920

Edition limited to 1 50 *copies*

LONDON: PRINTED AT THE CHISWICK PRESS
TOOKS COURT, CHANCERY LANE

CONTENTS

ILLUSTRATIONS

Three-quarter scale Facsimiles of the five types of the Maps accompanying this volume

MAP TITLES

A reduced facsimile of the Title and Cartouche of each of the Nineteen Maps will be found as an ornamental head-piece to the Chapter describing the same

PREFACE

THE first Edition of this little Essay was published in 1905, and its aims and objects are perhaps best described by quoting from the original Preface.

"Having recently acquired a copy of the original Philadelphia "edition of Lewis Evans' Map of the Middle British Colonies in America, pub-"lished in 1755, together with his accompanying descriptive *Analysis*[1] of the "same, I was tempted to read the book and examine the map. Recognizing "some familiar features in the map, I compared it with the one in Pownall's "*Topographical Description*[2] of 1776, and was surprised to find that, although "twenty-one years apart in date, both were printed from the very same copper-"plate, although the latter contains some important additions and alterations.

"The text of Evans' *Analysis* was also found to be largely quoted as such "by Pownall in his *Topographical Description*. But on reading Pownall's "Preface I was greatly struck with the forcible protests he makes concerning "a certain piratical issue of Evans' map, said to have been made by Jefferys in "London soon after the original came over from Philadelphia in 1755, and "which piracy was then still current.

"I was sufficiently interested to hunt up this piratical issue in the Map "Room of the British Museum and compare it with the original. In my search "for this particular piracy, several other states and editions were discovered, "and between the British Museum collection and my own I was fortunately "able to identify no less than ten different issues, but it is by no means certain "that others may not yet come to light.

"The following Essay comprises the information acquired during the "search." —*January*, 1905.

My prognostication that it was by no means certain that other editions might not come to light, has been more than amply fulfilled, for during the intervening fifteen years no less than eight more

---

[1] *Vide* full title, p. 6.   [2] *Vide* full title, p. 33.

distinct issues have been identified, bringing the total up to eighteen. Even now finality is by no means assured.

Furthermore I have had the extreme good fortune to run across a copy of Evans' earlier Map of 1749. As this is excessively rare and very little known, I have had it reproduced in facsimile (slightly reduced), and for the purpose of comparison I have added a similar facsimile of the original issue of his later and better known Map of 1755.

This Second Edition includes descriptive Notes on the Map of 1749, and on the additional eight derivatives from that of 1755. The Notes on the ten issues described in the First Edition, have been revised and corrected, and such additions made as became necessary by the incorporation of the further eight intermediate editions in their proper chronological sequence.

For the purposes of illustration and comparison, I have included facsimiles (also slightly reduced) of Pownall's re-issue in 1776 of the original Philadelphia plate of 1755 enlarged and corrected, as well as the first issues of the two piratical plates, published respectively by Kitchin and Bowles, from which two types all the other later editions emanated.

As the expense would not permit the reproduction of the whole series of nineteen maps, I have contented myself by giving in reduced facsimile the title-cartouche of each issue, which will be found as an ornamental headpiece to the Chapter describing the same.

It is not the intention in these Notes to give a general biographical sketch of the life of Evans, but rather to trace the curious cartographical ramifications in England, emanating from his Map of 1755 during the succeeding period of more than half a century.

There is little material to be found in England relating to Evans personally, apart from brief notices in various biographical dictionaries. For the purpose of this Essay suffice it therefore briefly to say—that he was born about 1700—that he became a Surveyor in Pennsylvania, and made many journeys into the neighbouring Colonies,[1] and was frequently employed in surveying lands purchased from the Indians—that he collected a vast store of information during his travels and from his surveys, from which he compiled a Map of the Middle Colonies and the adjacent countries of the Indians to the North and West—that the First Edition of his Map was published in 1749, and the second in 1755, the latter accompanied by an explanatory Essay entitled *Analysis of a general Map of the Middle British Colonies in America*—that some expressions of opinion contained in this pamphlet which appeared to uphold the claims of France to Fort Frontenac, and some supposed errors in the Map, brought him into controversy with an anonymous writer who attacked him in Gaine's *New York Mercury* in January 1756—that he immediately replied to the same in a second Essay [2] published the same month, in which he defended his opinions on the French claims and the accuracy of his Map—and that he died shortly afterwards (12 June 1756), whilst under imprisonment for a libel on Robert Hunter Morris, Lieutenant Governor of Pennyslvania.

Beyond these general facts, any further biographical details I have been enabled to gather in the course of my cartographical investigations, will be found incorporated in the following Notes.

HENRY N. STEVENS.

March 1920.

[1] *Vide* one of his Journals printed by Pownall in *Topographical Description* 1776, Appendix No. V.
[2] *Vide* full title, p. 11.

A COMPARATIVE ACCOUNT OF THE ORIGINAL EDITIONS OF LEWIS EVANS' MAPS OF 1749 AND 1755 AND THEIR DERIVATIVES

I

THE ORIGINAL MAP OF 1749

THE title, as given in reduced facsimile in the headpiece above, is placed centrally at the top, just inside the double border, in a slightly ornamented cartouche, and occupies a space 12¾ inches long by 1¾ deep. The imprint, *Publifhed by Lewis Evans March 25 1749 according to Act of Parliament* is in the top left corner, immediately to the left of the title. The engraver's name, *L. Hebert fculp[t]*, is in the lower right corner outside the border line. The whole Map measures 19¼ × 25¼ inches[1] between the outside border lines, and is drawn on the scale of fifteen English miles to the inch. (*Vide facsimile* No. I.)

The top border shows the Longitude East and West from the prime meridian of Philadelphia, the line of which runs down the map a little to the right of the centre. The corresponding Longitude, West from London, is shown in the bottom border. On page 1 of his *Analysis*[2] of 1755, Evans gives the following interesting reasons for having chosen Philadelphia as the prime meridian:

"The Britifh Settlements are done, for the greater Part, from actual "Surveys. The Latitudes of many Places taken with good Inftruments, and "the Longitudes of Philadelphia and Bofton, obferved by different Perfons,

---

[1] In all the measurements herein given, the first is taken from left to right as the map lies before the observer, and the second from top to bottom.

[2] *Vide* p. 5, *infra.*

B

"and well agreeing, give a Foundation for the Projection of the Map. And
"as Philadelphia is a fine City, fituate near the Center of the Britifh Dominions
"on this Continent; and whether inferior to others in Wealth, or Number of
"Houfes, or not, it far excels in the Progrefs of Letters, mechanic Arts, and
"the public Spirit of its Inhabitants; I thought Reafon fufficient for paying it
"the particular Diflinction of making it the firft Meridian of America. And a
"Meridian here I thought the more neceffary, that we may determine the
"Difference of the Longitude of Places by Menfuration; a Method far excel-
"ling the beft aftronomical Obfervations; and as we may be led into feveral
"Errors by always reckoning from remote Meridians. . . . Near the Weftern
"Extremity [of the City] is the Statehoufe, the Spot propofed for my Meridian
"to be drawn through."

This map is so rare that little is known about it beyond what
Evans himself tells us in a long legend engraved upon it in the lower
left corner. As this refers to the sources of information, it may be as
well to quote it in full, in the hope that some of the Surveys and Maps
mentioned, which at present do not seem to be known, may perhaps
be traced and identified.

"I have omitted Nothing in my Power to render this Map as complete as
"poffible. And tho' no Diftance could be taken but by actual Menfuration
"(the Woods being yet fo thick) I can declare it to be more exact than could
"be well expected; but the Merit is far from being my own. To fill thofe
"Parts, where our Settlements and Difcoveries have not yet extended to, I have
"introduced fev¹ ufeful Remarks in Phyfics & Commerce. The Generofity of
"fev¹ Gentⁿ efpecially Mefsˢ Nichˢ Scull, Jofeph Reeves, Geo. Smith, John
"Lydius, & Nichˢ Stilwil, in furnifhing me with their Draughts & Difcoveries
"demands my Thanks and Acknowledgment. I have been affifted with the
"Draughts of many other Gent. that I had not immediate Acquaintance with,
"amongft which the MS. & printed Maps of the Northern Neck, Mr. Law-
"rence's new Divifion Line of Jerfey & Mʳ Noxon's Map of the Three lower
"Counties were not the leaft remarkable. The Collections of Ifaac Norris and
"James Alexander Efqˢ were of fingular Service to me, as containing Variety
"of Draughts not to be met with elfewhere. And the greateft Part of New
"York Province is owing to the honourable Cadwallader Colden Efqʳ."

The "useful Remarks in Physics and Commerce" referred to
above are in long legends, engraved in blank spaces, mostly in the
North-West portion of the Map, and relate to the extremes of the
Barometer and Thermometer at Philadelphia;—the progress of Storms;
—Navigation of Delaware and other Bays and Rivers;—Ice;—Fogs;
Thunder, Lightning and Electricity;—Land and Sea Winds;—Clouds;

—Notes on Longitude, etc. etc. Near the centre of the Map is a very long description of " the Endless Mountains," and in the lower right corner is a Table for calculating the distances between numerous places of importance.

Perhaps the most interesting and important of all these legends is the one relating to Lightning and Electricity. Governor Pownall, in his *Topographical Description of North America*,[1] published in 1776, seems to suggest on page 45 that Franklin's discoveries in Electricity were based on the observations of Evans. Pownall's exact words are worth quoting :

> " I cannot cloſe theſe Obſervations without tranſcribing from Lewis Evans's
> " Map of Pennſylvania, New York, and New Jerſey, printed at Philadelphia
> " 1749, the following curious, at that Time novel and very curious, philoſophic
> " Propoſitions; not only as they point to very ingenious Experiments, but as
> " they ſhew what Progreſs *He* had made in that ſingular Branch of Philoſophy,
> " *Electricity*, at a Period when even the firſt Philoſophers were but Empirics in it.
>   ' All our Storms, ſays he, begin to Leeward; thus a North Eaſt Storm
> ' will be a Day sooner in Virginia than in Boſton. Thunder never happens
> ' but by the Meeting of Sea and Land Clouds, the Sea Clouds coming,
> ' *freighted with Electricity*, and meeting others leſs ſo, the Equilibrium is
> ' reſtored by *Snaps of Lightning*; and the more oppoſite the Winds and the
> ' larger and compacter the Clouds, the more dreadful are theſe Shocks : The
> ' Sea Clouds thus ſuddenly bereft of that univerſal Element of Repellancy,
> ' contract, and their Waters guſh down in Torrents.'
> " His Philoſophy here is not perfectly juſt, though it contains very ſhrewd
> " leading Theorems, of which, with a true and painful philoſophic Courſe of
> " Experiments, Dr. FRANKLIN elicited the real Truth."

When one considers the vast tract of country covered by this Map (much of it unsettled and unexplored), and the obstacles in the way of easy transit whilst surveying in wooded and mountainous districts, the extreme difficulty of making a Map on so small a scale as fifteen miles to the inch with any pretensions to accuracy, may readily be realized. And yet the general errors appear to have been relatively very small, for in the *Analysis* which accompanies Evans' Map of 1755, he says on page 3 :

" A Map I publiſhed of Pennſylvania, New Jerſey, New York and

[1] *Vide* p. 33, *infra*. Cf. also [Life of] *Thomas Pownall*, by C. A. W. Pownall. *London*, Henry Stevens, Son, and Stiles, 1908, p. 279.

"Delaware, in 1749, is reduced to a smaller Scale in this, and forms thoſe
"four Colonies. The Errors are rectified, the principal of which were, Albany
"placed too far North, Shamokin too far Weſt, and all the Route thence to
"Oſwego five Miles altogether too much North; beſides ſeveral Imperfections
"in Places which later Obſervations and Diſcoveries have given us Knowledge
"of. In the firſt Impreſſion of my former Map I committed ſome Miſtakes in
"the Names of Places, near the Entrance of Delaware Bay on the Weſt Side,
"and in my Attempt to rectify them, in the ſecond Edition, did but add to the
"Confuſion. I have ſince had an Opportunity of making a thorough Enquiry
"into this Affair, and conclude, that the Names which the Places thereabouts
"are now called by, and are the ſame as laid down in my General Map,[1] are
"the only Names they ever had, and ſtill retain amongſt thoſe acquainted
"with them; as Lewes, Whore-kill Road, Cape Hinlopen, Falſe Cape, and
"Fenwick's Iſland. . . . All muſt admit that the preſent Names are rightly
"laid down," &c. &c.

This statement seems to imply that there were two issues or
impressions of the Map of 1749, but as the one here reproduced in
facsimile is the only edition as yet seen by the writer, he is unable to
describe the differences. It will be observed by a comparison of the
facsimiles of the Maps of 1749 and 1755, that the above-mentioned
names are the same in both, except that the Map of 1749 does not
extend sufficiently far South to include *Fenwick's Island.* If anyone
possesses, or knows the whereabouts of a copy of the Map of 1749 of
a different impression to the one here reproduced, he will greatly oblige
the writer by communicating particulars to him.

Some further references to the Map of 1749 will be found in the
Notes describing the additions and corrections made in the Map of
1755.

[1] *I.e.,* the Map of 1755, our No. II.

II

The Original Map of 1755 [1]

WHEN on 23 June 1755, Evans published at Philadelphia his famous *General Map of the Middle British Colonies in America*, he little dreamed that it was destined to become the prototype of most of the Maps of North America published in England during the next half century. Seventeen of these direct derivatives are described in the following chapters, but the influence of this Map is clearly to be traced in numerous others, which are not merely slavish copies.

In his Map of 1749 Evans, as we have seen, had filled up the blank spaces with lengthy legends describing his sources of information, including numerous " useful Remarks in Physics and Commerce." In the present more pretentious and comprehensive Map the legends are comparatively few and short, but in a three-line Note in the bottom left corner, he says: " Want of Room obliges me to refer my Thanks " to the many Gentlemen who favoured me with their Notes in the " Performance, to the ANALYSIS."

This *Analysis*, which accompanied the Map, was issued in the form of a closely printed quarto pamphlet (iv + 32 *pp.*). It was printed by B. Franklin and D. Hall at Philadelphia in 1755, and two editions appeared the same year. The fact that they are distinct impressions

---

[1] *Vide facsimile* No. II.

throughout, shows that there must have been sufficient demand for
the work, to have exhausted the first edition and made a reprint
necessary. As the two editions are very similar in appearance, it is
more than likely the second was printed from standing type corrected;
but there are sufficient differences on every page to clearly indicate the
entire reimpression. The second edition may readily be detected by
the printers' mark on the first and third pages of each sheet, *viz.*, a
small figure 2 beneath the last line of text (but above the footnotes),
half an inch in from the left margin. This mark is found on pages 1,
3, 9, 11, 17, 19, 25, and 27. More or less alteration has been made
on every page, but the following will serve for easy identification.
The first edition has no sectional headings on pages 6 and 11, whereas
in the second, headings have been inserted, *The Face of the Country*
on page 6 between lines 7 and 8, and *The Boundaries of the Con-
federates, &c.*, on page 11 in the centre.

It was probably due to the suggestion of Thomas Pownall (to
whom the Map is dedicated, and who was in Philadelphia at the time
of publication),[1] that some copies of the Map and the *Analysis* were
also prepared for the English market, for certain copies of both the
First and Second Editions bear the additional line in the imprint,
"and sold by J. & R. Dodsley in Pall-Mall, London." There are
therefore four distinct issues of the title-page of the *Analysis*, viz., the
First and Second Editions with the imprint of B. Franklin and
D. Hall alone, and the First and Second Editions with the additional
Dodsley imprint. There do not appear to be any other variations
between the Philadelphia and London issues of either edition.

The full Title of the First Edition reads as follows:

" *Geographical, Historical,* | *Political, Philosophical and Mechanical* | *ESSAYS* |.
" The First, Containing | an | ANALYSIS | Of a General Map of the | MIDDLE
" BRITISH COLONIES | in | America; | And of the Country of the
" Confederate Indians: | A Description of the Face of the Country; | The
" Boundaries of the Confederates; | and the | Maritime and Inland Naviga-
" tions of the several Rivers | and Lakes contained therein. | By Lewis Evans. |
" *Philadelphia:* | Printed by B. Franklin, and D. Hall. MDCCLV. |

[1] *Vide op. cit., Thomas Pownall*, 1908, p. 58.

The Map is usually folded up and placed at the end of the *Analysis*, but is sometimes, though rarely, found separately in un-folded state. Copies of the *Analysis* frequently occur without the original Map, in substitution of which one or other of the pirated London editions is oftentimes inserted. Care should therefore be taken when purchasing a copy of the *Analysis* to see that it contains the genuine original edition of the Map *Engraved by Ja' Turner in Philadelphia*, and bearing Evans' imprint in the bottom right-hand corner. The pirated copies of the Map are of little use for reading-in with the *Analysis*, for they do not contain the lettered references cor-responding to the side-notes in the text, indicating the positions of the places mentioned. Furthermore they are defective and misleading in their delineations, as pointed out by Pownall in his *Topographical Description* of 1776.[1]

The original Map has the title in an ornamental cartouche placed at the top in the centre, just below the border lines. *Vide* the reduced facsimile in the headpiece to this chapter. Below the cartouche is a scale of 150 English miles, which works out at thirty-six miles to the inch. Immediately to the left of the bottom of the cartouche is the engraver's imprint, *Engraved by Ja' Turner in Philadelphia*. In the right-hand bottom corner, just inside the border line, is the publisher's imprint in two lines. *Published according to Act of Parliament, by Lewis Evans. June 23. 1755. and / sold by* R. Dodsley, *in Pall-Mall,* LONDON, *& by the Author in* PHILADELPHIA./

In the upper left-hand corner is a Dedication to Pownall, with an elaborate Coat of his Arms,[2] so engraved as to appear to be on a separate piece of paper ($7\frac{5}{8}$ inches long by $2\frac{1}{2}$ high), pasted on the Map.

" *To the Honourable* Thomas Pownall *Esqr*. / *Permit me, Sir, to pay You* " *this Tribute of Gratitude,* / *for the great Assistance You have given me in this* "*Map; and to* / *assure the Public, that it has past the Examination of a Gentleman,* / "*whom I esteem the best Judge of it in America :* / *Your most obedient,* / *and most* " *humble Servant,* / L *Evans.* / "

Below the Dedication is an inset entitled *A Sketch of the remaining Part*

---

[1] *Vide* p. 36, *infra*.   [2] *Vide p.* 39, *infra, also the facsimile* No. II.

of Ohio R. &c., also engraved in such a manner as to appear to be a separate piece of paper pasted on the main map, and occupying a space of $5\frac{1}{4}$ inches wide by $6\frac{1}{2}$ high. About an inch inside the bottom border of the main map, just to the right of the centre, is an inscription engraved so as to represent a label three inches long by half an inch high, *For a particular Map of VIRGINIA the Reader is referred to that by* Fry *and* Jefferson, *publish'd by Mr Jefferys near Charing Cross,* LONDON, *in* 1751. There are also several legends in different parts of the Map, relating mostly to the Indians and the nature of the country, but the special features mentioned in detail above will be sufficient for identification and comparison, even without consulting the accompanying facsimile.

The whole map measures within the outside border lines $26\frac{1}{8}$ inches by $19\frac{3}{8}$. Certain extensions in North Carolina at the bottom and in New France at the top, are carried through the double border right up to the outside line. The plate mark is about $\frac{1}{4}$ inch beyond the border lines, and the uncut sheet of paper measures about $29\frac{3}{4}$ by $21\frac{1}{2}$ inches. The top border shows the Longitudes East and West from Philadelphia, while the bottom border shows the Longitudes from London. Evans' reasons for adopting Philadelphia as his prime Meridian have already been given in the description of the map of 1749.[1]

For the purposes of easy reference the top border has each degree space marked with a small letter, a to s, commencing on the right, and the right-hand border has each degree space similarly marked with capital letters, A to K, commencing at the top. These lettered references correspond to similar letterings in the side-notes of the *Analysis*, thus easily indicating the positions of places mentioned in the descriptive text.

Turning now to the *Analysis*, Evans tells us in his Preface that—

" *The Map, that these Sheets accompany, and that they are intended to explain*
" *and supply, is presented to the Public, when a longer Time was indeed necessary*
" *to have given it the Degree of Correctness that was intended it. But the present*
" *Conjuncture of Affairs in America, and the generous Assistance of the Assembly of*

[1] *Vide* p. 1, *ante.*

" *Penſilvania, have brought it to Light, when the Public will, it is hoped, receive*
" *Advantages from it, that will render an Apology for its premature Publication*
" *needleſs; and think it worthy the Encouragement of a* BODY *who devote the*
" *Public Money to the Public Service.*"

The "present conjuncture of affairs" no doubt refers to the rapidly increasing encroachments of France on the back settlements, to which Evans draws particular attention in his *Analysis*. He especially points out the great advantages to the English Colonies of the Country on the Ohio and the Lakes, and urges the necessity for more general knowledge of the nature and position of those remote parts and of the various ways by which they may be reached, in order that the French may more easily be dispossessed. He then proceeds to explain the scope and details of his map, and particularly he points out the nature and sources of his information, and quotes his authorities for each part of the country when describing it.

On page 3 he explains that his former map of 1749 of Pennsylvania, New Jersey, New York, and Delaware, forms the basis of these four Colonies in the present map, but reduced to a smaller scale (actually from fifteen to thirty-six miles to the inch). He goes on to point out how the old errors of 1749 arose and how they have now been corrected, and from what sources the imperfections in that former map have now been supplied and completed, and the new map so extended as to include the new Eastern Colonies of Connecticut, Rhode Island, Massachusetts, and New Hampshire, also the Southern Colonies of Maryland and Virginia, and the Western Settlements in the Ohio Country, as well as the Country to the North, including Lakes Erie, Ontario and Champlain, and Part of New France.

These details occupy the first five pages of the *Analysis*. Pages 6 to 10 describe the face of the country and its general physical features. Due credit is given by name to the various explorers and travellers whose Surveys, Journals and Notes, have been largely used in the laying down of the Map, more particularly as regards the new and important country bordering on the Ohio River. Pages 11 to 16 treat of the boundaries of the Confederate Indian Nations, and the danger arising from their threatened alliance with the French in their encroachments on the back settlements. Pages 17 to 32 contain a description of the most considerable Rivers and the methods employed in their navigation, with notes on numerous cross-country routes to be made by means of portages, etc.

One has only to read Evans' *Analysis* to readily realize the extreme difficulty of making a map of this vast country on a small scale of about thirty-six miles to the inch on anything like correct lines. It is evident that he drew the map with the most conscientious desire for accuracy, and the *Analysis* reveals the extraordinary amount of information he had collected for the purpose. In his concluding remarks he makes some curious and slighting allusions to the ambitions of Massachusetts towards Independency, most interesting at this early date, and prophetic in the light of subsequent events. But the main object of his book seems to have been to direct particular attention to the advantages of a Colony on the Ohio and the retrieving of the country encroached on by the French.

Some copies of the map were probably issued in advance of the publication of the *Analysis*, for the map is stated in the imprint to have been published on June 23, 1755, whereas the Preface to the *Analysis* is dated August 9. In Evans' Essay, No. II,[1] published in 1756, he says on page 24:

"My map was begun engraving in November 1754 and finished "towards the end of June 1755, the pamphlet published August 9th "next following."

The map evidently excited considerable attention in the Colonies, and, according to what Governor Pownall says in 1776,[2] it was for a long time generally accepted as the standard authority for settling boundaries, purchases, etc., on account of the extreme care and accuracy with which it had been prepared. (*Vide* No. XIII, p. 35.)

As a further testimony to the accuracy of Evans' work, Captain

---

[1] *Vide* full title, pp. 11.
[2] *Topographical Description*, p. iv.

Thomas Hutchins may be quoted, who, in the Preface to his *Topo-graphical Description of Virginia,* published in 1778, says:

"It is fit also, that I should take notice, that in the account which
" I have given of several of the branches of the Ohio, and Alleghany
" rivers, I have adopted the words of the late ingenious Mr. Lewis
" Evans, as I found he had properly described them in the Analysis
" to his Map of the Middle Colonies."

Nevertheless, it is clear that the map and *Analysis* did not satisfy all parties, especially the Shirley faction, for in the *New York Mercury* for January 5th, 1756, appeared a letter with the following heading:

"Mr. Gaine. The following Letter from a Gentleman in New
" York to his Friend at Philadelphia is upon a subject of so much im-
" portance that I beg you'll give it a Place in your Paper."

The letter is dated 1st December 1755, and in it the writer accuses Evans of wrongfully stating in his *Analysis* the right of the French to the country on the North-West of the St. Lawrence River from Fort Frontenac to Montreal. He further characterizes him as diverting himself by setting false bounds to Provinces and Empires on his map, and he falls foul of Evans' conclusions generally.

Although this letter was only published in the *New York Mercury* of January 5th, Evans immediately replied to it at some length; answering and refuting his antagonist on all points in a pamphlet issued in similar style to the *Analysis* under the following title:

"*Geographical, Hiftorical,* | *Political, Philofophical and Mechanical* |
" ESSAYS. / Number II. Containing, / A / LETTER / *Reprefenting,* / the Impro-
" priety of fending Forces to *Virginia* : / The Importance of taking *Frontenac*; /
" And that the Prefervation of *Ofwego* was owing to General *Shirley's* / Proceed-
" ing thither. / And containing Objections to thofe Parts of *Evans's* General Map
" and / Analyfis, which relate to the *French* Title to Country, on the / North-
" Weft Side of the St. Laurence River, between Fort Frontenac / and Montreal,
" &c. / Publifhed in the New-York Mercury, No. 178, Jan. 5, 1756. / With an /
" Anfwer, / To fo much thereof as concerns the Public; / And the feveral Articles
" fet in a juft Light. / By Lewis Evans. / Philadelphia : / Printed for the Author;
" and Sold by him in Arch-Street : / And at New York by G. Noel, Bookfeller
" near Counts's Market. / MDCCLVI. / " [1]

[1] 4to, pp. 42 + (1).

In this pamphlet Evans reprints in full the letter from the *New York Mercury*. It will be observed that on the title he divides the writer's views into various sections.   In his second Chapter he discusses at length the question " How far General Shirley's Conduct was condu-
" cive to the preservation of Oswego." He develops a very strong negative argument to show that Sir William Johnson's victory over the French under Dieskau near Lake George,[1] thereby upsetting their plans, was the direct cause of the saving of Oswego, which would otherwise have been inevitably lost through the unpardonable conduct of General Shirley in so long delaying to put that important post in a position to resist all attacks.

Chapter III is " an enquiry into the advantages and disadvantages
" that would arise from the taking of Fort Frontenac." Chapter IV contains a long and exhaustive " explanation of the French Title to
" the Country on the North-west side of St. Lawrence River, between
" Fort Frontenac and Montreal." After quoting numerous authorities in support of his arguments, Evans concludes :

" I have thus related the Circumſtances which induced me to form the
" Opinion I publiſhed in my Analyſis in regard to the Right of the Country
" lying between Fort *Frontenac* and *Montreal,* on the North-weſt Side of
" *St. Laurence.* I am morally certain of every Circumſtance I have related ; if
" my Concluſions are wrong, I ſhould be glad of ſeeing the Point ſet in a better
" Light."

Altogether Evans seems to have had the best of the argument with the anonymous writer who attacked him in the *New York Mercury*.   He spiritedly holds to and defends the views given in his *Analysis,* and while asserting his entire loyalty to the Colonies and his desire to see the French dispossessed, he reasserts that his sole object was to set down on his map such boundaries as his information and

---

[1] For a most interesting account of this Battle *see* the Plan and Explanation published by Samuel Blodget, *A Prospective View of the Battle near Lake George on the 8ᵗʰ of Sepʳ 1755 between 2000 English with 250 Mohawks under the Command of Genˡ Johnson & 2500 French and Indians under the command of Genˡ Dieskau in which the English were victorious, captivating the French General with a number of his men killing 700 and putting the rest to flight. With an Explanation thereof containing a full though short History of that important affair.*   Reprinted and the Plan reproduced in facsimile with a prefatory Note by Henry N. Stevens, F.R.G.S. *London*: Henry Stevens, Son, and Stiles. 1911.

surveys led him to believe were correct, thus acting fairly and im-
partially to both sides. Although this pamphlet fills forty-two quarto
pages, the preface is dated 10 January 1756, only five days after the
publication of the letter in the *New York Mercury*.

The controversy thus raised over the French Title to Frontenac,
etc., brought Evans numerous enemies, for feeling ran high at the
time between the partisans of General Shirley and Sir William
Johnson. As an instance, the writer may mention that some years ago
he found in an old Atlas, a leaf of contemporary manuscript attached
to a copy of one of the London reprints of Evans' map, which he
ventures to quote, not as any real reflection on the character of
Evans, but merely to show how partisan feeling could descend to
vulgar abuse of a worthy man even after his death.

"Evans Map & firſt Analyſis, publiſhed 1755, & yᵗ paſt in favour of ye
"french Claim to Frontenac was attacked by 2 Papers in ye New York
"Mercury Janʸ 1756. This occaſioned his publiſhing a 2ⁿᵈ Pamphlet ye next
"Spring in wᶜʰ he endeavours to ſupport his Map.—He was a Man in low
"Circumſtances, in his Temper precipitate, of violent paſſions, great Vanity &
"rude Manners. He pretended to ye Knowledge of everything, & yet had
"very little learning. By his inquiſitive turn he filled his Head with a conſider-
"able Collection of Materials, & a Perſon of more Judgment than he had,
"might for a few Days receive advantages from his Converſation. He piqued
"himſelf much upon his 2 Maps wᶜʰ are however juſtly chargeable with many
"errors. His ignorance of Languages is viſible both in them & in ye 2
"Pamphlets of his Analyſis, ye laſt of wᶜʰ is ſtuffed with groundleſs aſperſions
"on Governor Shirley, who deſerves ſo well of theſe Colonies yᵗ on yᵗ accᵗ &
"to weaken ye authority of a Map prejudicial to his Majeſtys rights, I beg ye
"Readers excuſe for this infraction of ye old Rule, *De mortuis nil niſi bonum*.
"He died at New York June 12 1756 under an arreſt for a groſs Slander agˢᵗ
"Mʳ Morris Governor of Penſylvania."

As against this scurrilous anonymous opinion one has only to
quote Franklin and Pownall in refutation. Franklin, in his answer in
1772 to Lord Hillsborough's adverse Report on the proposed Grant
to Thomas Walpole and his Associates of a tract of Lands on the
Ohio River, speaks of Evans as "a gentleman of great American
knowledge," and quotes his map as authoritative.[1] Pownall thought
sufficiently well of him to accept the dedication of his Map in

---

[1] Sparks, *Franklin*, iv, 326.

1755,[1] and after more than twenty years, pays a glowing tribute to its great accuracy, based on the experience gained in the meantime in its use on the spot as well as in England.[2]

At the time of the publication of Evans' second Essay, considerable annoyance was being caused to the Home Government by the persistent encroachments of the French on the back settlements. It is not surprising, therefore, to find that the matter aroused extensive public interest in England. The desire for information doubtless caused considerable demand for those copies of Evans' Map and *Analysis* which had been sent over from Philadelphia for sale in London by R. and J. Dodsley. The subject was evidently attracting such great public notice, that instead of copies of Evans' second Essay being sent over from America for sale in London, that pamphlet was immediately reprinted there by R. and J. Dodsley,[3] probably at the instigation of Governor Pownall, who happened to be in England during the first half of the year 1756.

The work is briefly noticed in the *Monthly Review* for September 1756. The Reviewer holds that Evans has replied to the Letter in the *New York Mercury* of 5 January 1756, " with the appearance of " much solidity of argument, as well as honesty of intention. He was " certainly a sensible man, a good geographer (so far at least as con-" cerns that part of the world he treats of) and a true friend to his " country; so that his death may justly be deemed a public loss."

From the extensive titles of the two Essays which Evans published in 1755 and 1756, it is is evident that he contemplated continuing the series, but unfortunately he died in June 1756. From the Preface to his *Analysis* it would seem that he intended issuing maps of the separate Colonies on a larger scale, in which he would be able to include certain sectional and physical features which he was compelled to omit from his *Map of the Middle British Colonies* for want of space. He also mentions in the Preface that the Time of High Water at the Full and Change of the Moon, and the Variation of the

---

[1] *Vide* p. 6 *supra* and 39 *infra*. [2] *Vide* p. 35, *infra*.
[3] 4to, 35 pp.

Magnetic Needle are laid down in the Map. " But as these deserve
" particular Explanations, I have for want of Room, concluded to treat
" of them at large in a separate Essay." It is to be feared that his
death within a year of the expression of these intentions prevented the
realization of any of them, to the great loss of posterity.

A general MAP *of the*
MIDDLE BRITISH COLONIES in AMERICA:
Viz. *VIRGINIA, MARYLAND, DELAWARE, PENSILVANIA,*
NEW-JERSEY, NEW-YORK, CONNECTICUT and *RHODE-ISLAND;*
Of AQUANISHUONIGY *the Country of the* Confederate Indians
Comprehending AQUANISHUONIGY *proper, their Places of Residence,*
OHIO and THUCHSOCHRUNTIE *their Deer Hunting Countries,*
COUCHSACHRAGE and SKANIADARADE *their Beaver Hunting Countries,*
of the LAKES ERIE, ONTARIO *and* CHAMPLAIN,
And of Part of NEW-FRANCE:
Wherein is also shewn the antient and present SEATS of the
Indian Nations; *carefully copied from the Original Publish'd at*
Philadelphia. By M.r Lewis Evans 1755. *with*
some Improvements By I. Gibson.

III

1756. THE KITCHIN PIRACY

EVANS' Map, as published in London by R. and J. Dodsley in 1755, had in the meantime attracted the attention of a rival map publisher, T. Kitchin, who piratically copied, re-engraved, and published it in 1756, professedly with improvements. Pownall was apparently unaware of this issue by Kitchin, for he does not refer to it, but in his *Topographical Description* of 1776 he writes as if Jefferys was the author of the piracy, whereas in reality he only reissued in 1758 Kitchin's plate of 1756. Pownall says: " this plagiarism was falsely sold as " Evans's map improved; by which that very laborious and ingenious " but poor man was deprived of the Benefit of his Work."[1] The title reads as in the headpiece above. To say that this Map is carefully copied from the Original is a libel on Evans, as will be seen in our description of No. XIII, and from the facsimile[2] accompanying this volume. The Dedication to Pownall is omitted, and the resulting space is filled by the scale of 200 miles and by two descriptive paragraphs of text, the third and eighth from the Preface to the *Analysis*.

[1] *Vide* p. 36, *infra.*   [2] No. III.

16

Several of the Notes in the original map, relating personally to Evans, are entirely omitted, and their places filled with other notes taken wholly, or adapted, from the *Analysis*. The ornamental cartouche is of different design from the original. In the right-hand lower corner is the imprint, " *Sold by T. Kitchin Engraver & Printseller at the Star opposite Ely Gate Holborn. 1756. Price 2s.*" The Index letters in the margins are omitted. The size is slightly different from the original, being 26¼ by 19 within the outer border lines. The extensions in North Carolina at the bottom and in New France at the top are carried through the double border, right up to the outside line, exactly as in the original. Numerous differences (mostly erroneous) in the interior details of the country are manifest, to which reference will be found in Pownall's description of Jefferys' re-issue of this same plate. (*Vide* No. XIII, p. 37).

The I. Gibson mentioned on the title of this issue seems to have been a map draughtsman and engraver of some repute, for his name is to be found attached to many maps, mostly undated, but presumably between 1750 and 1780. At the end of the *Atlas Minimus*, published by J. Newbery in 1758, is an advertisement in which he gives his name and address as " J.[1] Gibson, Engraver No. 18 George's Court, Clerkenwell." His name appears frequently as engraver in conjunction with Eman Bowen, Geographer to his Majesty.

[1] Although Gibson's initial is given as I on Evans' map, the name John is frequently found on other maps.

IV

1758 JEFFERYS' RE-ISSUE OF KITCHIN'S PLATE

IN 1758 Kitchin's plate seems to have passed into the possession of Thomas Jefferys, the famous map publisher of Charing Cross, for in that year we find the map re-issued with exactly the same title as Kitchin's (see above) but with an alteration in the imprint in the lower right-hand corner, which now reads, *Sold by T. Jefferys, Charing Cross 1758. Price 2s. 6d.* The inherent defects common to both the Kitchin and Jefferys issues are fully described by Governor Pownall in his *Topographical Description* of 1776. (*Vide* No. XIII, p. 37.)

Very little difference is to be observed between the issues of 1756 and 1758, but a number of new Forts on the back settlements are added in this latter, *e.g.*, Forts Littleton, Shirley, Granville, Shipenock, Nominack, William Henry, Edward, Ticonderoga, etc., etc. Fort du Quesne, which was marked simply "F. du Quesne" in the 1756 plate, is now lettered "F^t du Quesne *Destroy'd* 1758 now called Pittsburg."

The accompanying facsimile [1] of Kitchin's map will serve to illustrate this issue, as both are from the same plate, and are exactly the same in size and detail save for the altered imprint and the few additional names.

[1] No. III.

A General MAP *of the*
MIDDLE BRITISH COLONIES *in* AMERICA

Viz VIRGINIA MARYLAND DELAWARE PENSILVANIA NEW JERSEY NEW YORK
CONNECTICUT & RHODE ISLAND *of* AQUANISHUONIGY *the Country of the*
Confederate Indians *Comprehending* Aquanishuonigy *proper their Places of Resi-*
dence OHIO & THUCHSOCHRUNTIE *their Deer Hunting Countries* COUCHSACHRAGE
& SKANIADARADE *their Beaver Hunting Countries of the* LAKES Erie Ontario &
Champlain *And of Part of* NEW FRANCE *Wherein is also shewn the antient*
& present Seats of the Indian Nations *carefully copied from the*
Original Published at Philadelphia by Mr Lewis Evans.

V

c. 1760? AN ANONYMOUS PIRACY FROM THE KITCHIN-JEFFERYS
PIRACY

THIS is an entirely re-engraved plate. The title, as given
in reduced facsimile above, has no ornamental border,
and the map bears no imprint or date. Although stated
in the title to be "carefully copied from the original
published at Philadelphia by Mr. Lewis Evans," it is clearly nothing
of the sort, for it has all the inherent defects pointed out by Pownall
in his *Topographical Description* as appertaining to the Jefferys' piracy.
(*Vide* No. XIII, p. 37.) In fact it is nothing more nor less than an abject
copy from the Kitchin-Jefferys plate, presumably a piracy, for it has
the same legends which Kitchin had inserted, and which do not appear
on Evans' original map at all, but were taken or adapted from the
Analysis. The size of the plate is $25\frac{1}{2}$ by $19\frac{3}{8}$ inches within the outside border lines. The scale of 200 miles, which in the Kitchin-
Jefferys plate equalled $5\frac{3}{8}$ inches, is now reduced to $5\frac{1}{2}$. Owing to the
increase in the height to $19\frac{3}{8}$ inches, and a reduction in the width of
the double border, the extensions in North Carolina and New France
(which in the Kitchin-Jefferys plate ran through the double border up
to the outer line) are now kept within the inner line. See the accompanying facsimile (No. V).

This map is clearly of later date than Jefferys' issue of 1758,
because it includes the additional names of the Forts in the back
settlements which Jefferys had inserted, as mentioned in our description of his plate in the previous Chapter. The date may therefore

19

A general MAP of the
MIDDLE BRITISH COLONIES in AMERICA:
Viz. VIRGINIA, MARYLAND, DELAWARE, PENSILVANIA,
NEW-JERSEY, NEW-YORK, CONNECTICUT and RHODE-ISLAND;
of AQUANISHUONIGY the Country of the Confederate Indians
Comprehending AQUANISHUONIGY proper, their Places of Residence,
OHIO and THUCHSOCHRUNTIE their Deer Hunting Countries,
COUCHSACHRAGE and SKANIADARADE their Beaver Hunting Countries
Of the LAKES ERIE, ONTARIO and CHAMPLAIN,
And of Part of NEW-FRANCE:
Wherein is also shewn the antient and present SEATS of the
Indian Nations, carefully copied from the Original Publish'd at
Philadelphia, By Mr Lewis Evans 1755, with
some Improvements By I. Gibson.

IV

1758. JEFFERYS' RE-ISSUE OF KITCHIN'S PLATE

IN 1758 Kitchin's plate seems to have passed into the possession of Thomas Jefferys, the famous map publisher of Charing Cross, for in that year we find the map re-issued with exactly the same title as Kitchin's (*see above*) but with an alteration in the imprint in the lower right-hand corner, which now reads, *Sold by T. Jefferys, Charing Cross* 1758. *Price* 2ˢ : 6ᵈ. The inherent defects common to both the Kitchin and Jefferys issues are fully described by Governor Pownall in his *Topographical Description of* 1776. (*Vide* No. XIII, p. 37).

Very little difference is to be observed between the issues of 1756 and 1758, but a number of new Forts on the back settlements are added in this latter, *e.g.*, Forts Littleton, Shirley, Granville, Shipeconk, Nominack, William Henry, Edward, Ticonderoga, etc., etc. Fort du Quesne, which was marked simply " F. du Quesne" in the 1756 plate, is now lettered "Fᵗ du Quesne *Destroy'd* 1758 *now called* Pittsburg."

The accompanying facsimile [1] of Kitchin's map will serve to illustrate this issue, as both are from the same plate, and are exactly the same in size and detail save for the altered imprint and the few additional names.

[1] No. III.

A General MAP *of the*

MIDDLE BRITISH COLONIES *in* AMERICA

Viz VIRGINIA MARYLAND DELAWARE PENSILVANIA NEW JERSEY NEW YORK
CONNECTICUT & RHODE ISLAND *of* AQUANISHUONIGY *the Country of the*
Confederate Indians *Comprehending* Aquanishuonigy *proper their Places of Resi-*
dence OHIO & TIUCHSOCHRUNTIE *their Deer Hunting Countries* COUCHSACHRAGE
& SHANIADARADE *their Beaver Hunting Countries of the* LAKES Erie Ontario &
Champlain *And of Part of* NEW FRANCE *Th herein is also shewn the antient*
& present Seats *of the* Indian Nations *carefully copied from the*
Original Publish'd at Philadelphia by Mr. Lewis Evans.

V

c. 1760? AN ANONYMOUS PIRACY FROM THE KITCHIN-JEFFERYS PIRACY

THIS is an entirely re-engraved plate. The title, as given in reduced facsimile above, has no ornamental border, and the map bears no imprint or date. Although stated in the title to be "carefully copied from the original published at Philadelphia by Mr. Lewis Evans," it is clearly nothing of the sort, for it has all the inherent defects pointed out by Pownall in his *Topographical Description* as appertaining to the Jefferys' piracy. (*Vide* No. XIII, p. 37.) In fact it is nothing more nor less than an abject copy from the Kitchin-Jefferys plate, presumably a piracy, for it has the same legends which Kitchin had inserted, and which do not appear on Evans' original map at all, but were taken or adapted from the *Analysis*. The size of the plate is $25\frac{1}{2}$ by $19\frac{5}{8}$ inches within the outside border lines. The scale of 200 miles, which in the Kitchin-Jefferys plate equalled $5\frac{5}{8}$ inches, is now reduced to $5\frac{1}{4}$. Owing to the increase in the height to $19\frac{5}{8}$ inches, and a reduction in the width of the double border, the extensions in North Carolina and New France (which in the Kitchin-Jefferys plate ran through the double border up to the outer line) are now kept within the inner line. See the accompanying facsimile (No. V).

This map is clearly of later date than Jefferys' issue of 1758, because it includes the additional names of the Forts in the back settlements which Jefferys had inserted, as mentioned in our description of his plate in the previous Chapter. The date may therefore be any time after 1758 and before 1763? The mention of *New France* in the title, and the lettering *Part of New France* on the map itself, would seem to indicate definitely that it was issued prior to the Peace with France in 1762-3, after which event the name *New France* was no longer current, on account of the cession of that Country to Great Britain, when the name *Canada* came into more general usage.

The publisher of this plate is unknown, but there can be little doubt that it emanated from one or other of the two current houses of Bowles, for subsequent states of the very same plate, re-issued from time to time with alterations, during the next forty years or so, as described hereinafter,[1] all bear the imprint of either *John Bowles*, *Carington Bowles*, or *Bowles and Carver*. At the time indicated the two houses of Bowles seem to have been carried on under the names of Thomas Bowles in St. Paul's Churchyard and John Bowles at the Black Horse in Cornhill. Although they were brothers the businesses seem to have been conducted independently. Some further particulars of the Bowles Family will be found in Chapter VII.

Having regard to the fact that there is no border to the title and no imprint, and that the impression is clear and sharp, the copy here described (which is the only one yet seen by the writer) may very possibly be a proof from an unfinished plate. Possibly the plate was incomplete at the moment of the Peace, and was held over for a time, for not long afterwards it was published with the imprint of *John Bowles and Carington Bowles*, with the addition of an ornamental border to the title and a few alterations as described in Chapter VII.

[1] *Vide* Nos. VII, VIII, IX, XVI, XVII, XIX.

VI

1758-[1768?] SAYER AND JEFFERYS' RE-ISSUE OF NO. IV WITH ALTERATIONS

ALTHOUGH bearing the old date of 1758, it is fairly evident that this state was not issued till some years later, probably not till after the Peace of 1762-3. It will be observed by comparing the facsimile given above with that of No. IV, that there are considerable alterations in the title. The first nine lines are exactly the same, after which there are now seven new lines in place of the former last five. The omission of the words *And Part of New France* lends force to the suggestion that this state of the map was not issued till after the Peace. But although omitted from the title, the lettering *Part of New France* still remains on the map itself.

The imprint which in No. IV read *Sold by T. Jefferys, Charing Cross* 1758. *Price* 2s. 6d.—has now been altered. The words *Sold by* have been erased on the copper, and in place thereof the imprint has been extended to the left so as now to read *Sold by R. Sayer in Fleet street & T. Jefferys, Charing Cross* 1758. *Price* 2s. 6d., the Jefferys part and the date remaining unaltered.

One would suppose from the addition to the title that this map was really "corrected and improved," but as far as can be seen, the alterations on the old copper plate since the Jefferys issue of 1758 are infinitesimal. Even the Forts now stated to be added by Jefferys are all to be found in the first 1758 issue, when the improvements were claimed on the title to be the work of I. Gibson, whose name is now omitted altogether. The only alteration in the body of the map readily to be noticed, is that the lettering "Part of / New Hampshire," is now in two lines both on the East side of Connecticut River, while in the first 1758 issue it was in one line, the words *Part of* being on the West side of the River. The old inherent defects common to both the Kitchin and Jefferys issues (Nos. III & IV), as fully described by Pownall in his *Topographical Description of* 1776, still remain. (*Vide* No. XIII, p. 37.)

The present state of the plate is to be found in a Collection of Maps entitled *A general Topography of North America*, published by R. Sayer & T. Jefferys in 1768, in which work it is called for as No. 32 in the Table of Contents. But the Map was probably sold in its present form some years before 1768, for most of the Maps in the *Topography* are well known to have been issued separately at an anterior date. The inference may fairly be drawn that this state of the map was first issued some time between 1763 and 1768, but why the old date of 1758 should have been allowed to remain uncorrected it is impossible to say. The custom of re-issuing maps after alteration, but with dates uncorrected, or without any dates at all, is one of the most puzzling features to be reckoned with in the study of comparative cartography, and frequently leads to much confusion and many erroneous conclusions.

A *General* Map *of the*
MIDDLE BRITISH COLONIES *in* AMERICA

VII

c. 1765? A RE-ISSUE BY JOHN BOWLES AND CARINGTON BOWLES OF THE ANONYMOUS PLATE NO. V

 COMPARISON of the facsimile of the title as given above with that of No. V, shows that an ornamental border has now been added, numerous commas inserted between the names of the Provinces, etc., and an alteration made in the seventh and eighth lines by the omission of the words *And of Part of New France.* Immediately below the title border the imprint has been inserted, engraved in Roman characters, " London, " Printed for John Bowles at the Black Horſe in Cornhil & Carington " Bowles in Sᵗ Pauls Church Yard."

Very little alteration is to be observed in the map itself except that the lettering *Part of New France,* which in No. V was placed across the country to the North West of the River St. Lawrence, has now been deleted. The dotted line of the Magnetic Meridian, which in No. V showed only to the North of the compass star, is now extended South to the bottom border line. With these exceptions (unless there are some minor alterations which have escaped notice) the map is apparently the same in detail as No. V, and is undoubtedly printed from the same copper plate.

The date of issue is somewhat uncertain, but judging from the fact of the omission of the name *New France*, both from the title and the map itself, it was certainly after the Peace of 1762-3, so that the assigned date of *c.* 1765?, given in the heading above, is probably not far wrong. Moreover, Carington Bowles first appears in the London Directory in 1765 at the address St. Paul's Churchyard,[1] having apparently succeeded to the business of his uncle Thomas Bowles, who had presumably retired, for he died 15 April 1767. Carington Bowles was the son of John Bowles of the Black Horse in Cornhill, and from 1754 to 1763 we find the style was John Bowles and Son, after which it is simply John Bowles. Presumably after 1765 the two businesses were carried on for joint interest, as the names are frequently found in conjunction.

For the sake of comparison with some of the later re-issues of this plate hereinafter described, it may be mentioned that in the present map (as also in No. V) the Connecticut River extends only as far North as [Fort] No. 4 at Great Falls (43° 10′), and there is no long lettering CANADA in very large letters extending diagonally from Ohio right across Lakes Erie and Ontario, and there is no dotted boundary line across the latter.

---

[1] The succession of Carington Bowles to the St. Paul's Churchyard business may have been in 1764, but as there is no copy of any London Directory for that year in the British Museum, this cannot be verified. In 1763 the old name, Thomas Bowles, appears. For some of the genealogical details of the Bowles family given here and there in this Essay, the writer is indebted to an extract from a manuscript pedigree in the possession of Sir William Collins, printed in 1913 by Sir H. G. Fordham in the *Supplement* to his *Descriptive Catalogue of the Maps of the County of Hertfordshire*, issued in 1913, the same being an excerpt in separate pamphlet form from Vol. XV Part II of *Transactions of the Hertfordshire Natural History Society and Field Club*.

A General Map of the
MIDDLE BRITISH COLONIES IN AMERICA
Viz. VIRGINIA, MARYLAND, DELAWARE, PENSILVANIA, NEW JERSEY NEW YORK,
CONNECTICUT & RHODE ISLAND of AQUANISHUONIGY the Country of the
Confederate Indians Comprehending Aquanishnonigy proper: their Places of Resi-
dence, OHIO & THUCHSOCHRUNTIE their Deer Hunting Countries, COUCHSACHRAGE
& SKANIADARADE their Beaver Hunting Countries, of the LAKES ERIE
ONTARIO and CHAMPLAIN. Wherein is also shown the antient
& present Seats of the Indian Nations; carefully copied from the
Original Publishd at Philadelphia, by Mr Lewis Evans.

Printed for Carington Bowles, at Nº69 in St Pauls Church Yard London;
Publishd Jan.Iᵗʰ 1771

VIII

1771. CARINGTON BOWLES' RE-ISSUE OF JOHN BOWLES AND CARINGTON BOWLES' UNDATED PLATE No. VII

THE title of this issue is exactly the same as No. VII, but the imprint has been altered and dated, as shown in the facsimile above. There are two issues by Carington Bowles, both bearing the same date 1771, but exhibiting considerable differences, which fact has only recently come to the knowledge of the writer. This, the earlier state, appears to be exactly the same impression as No. VII, save for the difference in the imprint. If any alterations have been made in the Map itself, they are unimportant and so minute as to readily escape observation. The general description of No. VII applies equally to the present issue, where relevant, so need not be repeated here. The second issue with the same date, is described in the next chapter.

IX

[c. 1774?] CARINGTON BOWLES' SECOND ISSUE WITH DATE
1771

THE fact that there are two distinct impressions, both bearing the imprint of Carington Bowles, dated Jany 1 1771, has only very recently come to the knowledge of the writer. The title and imprint of this second state are exactly the same as the first (No. VIII), as are also the general features of the map, but three important alterations denote the distinct impression.

A long lettering CANADA in large capitals, $\frac{5}{16}$ths of an inch tall, has been added, and extends diagonally across the map for 16 inches, from Ohio through Lake Erie to the country North-East of Lake Ontario, the letters A and N falling in Lake Erie. A dotted boundary line is inserted across the centre of Lake Ontario from Fort Frontenac to Ochniagara Falls. The Connecticut River, which in Nos. V, VII, and VIII ended at [Fort] No. 4 and Great Falls at 43° 10′, is now carried up to 45°, above which is a dotted boundary line extending right up to the top border in continuation of the river.

In three copies examined of this issue, a coloured line, evidently intended to show the boundaries of Canada, had been added by hand. It runs down the printed dotted line in the North-East corner of the

Map as far as the head of Connecticut River at 45°, thence west-ward along that parallel till it cuts the River St. Lawrence, up that river to Fort Fontenac, across Lake Ontario on the printed dotted line, up Niagara River, across the eastern end of Lake Erie to the small river marked "deep," thence south to Beaver Creek and down the Ohio River till it runs off the Map in the South-West corner.

The date of this issue is somewhat uncertain, but having regard to the fact that the main features of the alterations made in it relate to the boundaries of Canada, it would be reasonable to suggest that it was published in 1774, at the time when the whole question of the boundaries and government of Canada was being debated in Parliament. The matter was settled that same year by an Act known as the *Quebec Act*, which provided that that part of Canada extending southward to the River Ohio and westward to the Mississippi, should be annexed to, and form part and parcel of the Province of Quebec.

A General Map of the
MIDDLE BRITISH COLONIES in AMERICA
Viz. VIRGINIA, MARYLAND, DELAWARE, PENSILVANIA, NEW JERSEY, NEW YORK,
CONNECTICUT & RHODE-ISLAND of AQUANISHUONIGY the Country of the
Confederate Indians Comprehending Aquanishuonigy proper their Places of Resi-:
dences OHIO & THUCHSOCHRUNTIE their Deer Hunting Countries, COUCHSACHRAGE
& SKANIADARADE their Beaver Hunting Countries, of the LAKES ERIE
ONTARIO and CHAMPLAIN. Wherein is alsoshown the antient
& present Seats of the Indian Nations; carefully copied from the
Original Publishd at Philadelphia, by Mr Lewis Evans.

Printed for Carington Bowles, at No 69 in St Pauls Church Yard London,
Publishd Jany 1 1771,

IX

[c. 1774?] CARINGTON BOWLES' SECOND ISSUE WITH DATE
1771

THE fact that there are two distinct impressions, both bearing the imprint of Carington Bowles, dated Jany 1 1771, has only very recently come to the knowledge of the writer. The title and imprint of this second state are exactly the same as the first (No. VIII), as are also the general features of the map, but three important alterations denote the distinct impression.

A long lettering CANADA in large capitals, $\frac{5}{16}$ths of an inch tall, has been added, and extends diagonally across the map for 16 inches, from Ohio through Lake Erie to the country North-East of Lake Ontario, the letters A and N falling in Lake Erie. A dotted boundary line is inserted across the centre of Lake Ontario from Fort Frontenac to Ochniagara Falls. The Connecticut River, which in Nos. V, VII, and VIII ended at [Fort] No. 4 and Great Falls at 43° 10′, is now carried up to 45°, above which is a dotted boundary line extending right up to the top border in continuation of the river.

In three copies examined of this issue, a coloured line, evidently intended to show the boundaries of Canada, had been added by hand. It runs down the printed dotted line in the North-East corner of the

Map as far as the head of Connecticut River at 45°, thence westward along that parallel till it cuts the River St. Lawrence, up that river to Fort Fontenac, across Lake Ontario on the printed dotted line, up Niagara River, across the eastern end of Lake Erie to the small river marked "deep," thence south to Beaver Creek and down the Ohio River till it runs off the Map in the South-West corner.

The date of this issue is somewhat uncertain, but having regard to the fact that the main features of the alterations made in it relate to the boundaries of Canada, it would be reasonable to suggest that it was published in 1774, at the time when the whole question of the boundaries and government of Canada was being debated in Parlia ment. The matter was settled that same year by an Act known as the *Quebec Act*, which provided that that part of Canada extending southward to the River Ohio and westward to the Mississippi, should be annexed to, and form part and parcel of the Province of Quebec.

X

1775. SAYER AND JEFFERYS' FIRST RE-ISSUE OF NO. VI

THE fact that there were two distinct issues by Sayer and Jefferys in 1775 has only recently been observed by the writer. The titles of both are exactly the same as No. VI, as may be seen by a comparison of the facsimiles given above and on page 29 (No. XI) with that of No. VI on page 21.

The imprint of this first issue, which is still in one line only, in the lower right-hand corner, is almost the same as that of No. VI, varying only in the date, which has been altered on the copperplate from 1758 to 1775. The imprint accordingly now reads : *Sold by R. Sayer in Fleet street & T. Jefferys, Charing Crofs* 1775 *Price* 2*ˢ* : 6*ᵈ*. If any alterations have been made in the Map itself they are unimportant and so minute as to defy easy detection. As to its general features the reader is referred to the descriptions of Nos. IV and VI.

In the account of the second issue of 1775 in the next chapter, reference will be found to Pownall's emphatic protests against Sayer's further use of this piratical and erroneous plate, which of course apply equally to the present issue.

XI

1775. SAYER AND JEFFERYS' SECOND RE-ISSUE OF No. VI IN THE SAME YEAR

THE title and general features of this second issue of 1775 are exactly the same as the first (No. X). The only alteration appears to be in the imprint in the lower right-hand corner. The date 1775 in the one-line imprint of the first issue has been erased on the copper-plate and the resulting space left blank. A second line was then inserted, so that the complete new imprint now reads, *Sold by R. Sayer in Fleet street & T. Jefferys, Charing Crofs.* Price 2ˢ:6ᵈ./*Publish'd as the Act directs 15 June 1775./*

This issue is found in the *American Atlas* published by *Sayer and Bennett*[1] in 1775, where it forms Map No. 18 in the Table of Contents. It will be observed that while the imprint on the map is *Sayer and Jefferys*, it is *Sayer and Bennett* on the title of the Atlas. It is not thought that Sayer and Jefferys were in actual partnership, though their names are often found in conjunction, but from different addresses. It is believed that the partnership of Sayer and Bennett

---

[1] This name is frequently found spelt with one t.

began in 1775, for the name Sayer appeared alone in the London Directory for 1774, and previously for many years.[1]

According to Pownall[2] the Jefferys plate came into the hands of Sayer in the course of trade by purchase.[3] Pownall vehemently protests against the further use of this plate, and Sayer withdrew it from the next edition of the *American Atlas* published in 1776, and substituted for it in the Table of Contents No. 18 a map of Lake Champlain including Lake George. The whole story is told in our description of Pownall's re-issue in 1776 of Evans' original plate of 1755 improved (*vide* No. XIII, page 37, *infra*).

But the old plate was by no means dead yet, in fact it survived and did duty for another thirty years or so, as will be seen later on (*vide* Nos. XIV, XV, and XVIII).

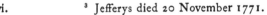

[1] It is generally supposed that Robert Sayer commenced business about 1745 at the *Golden Buck* in Fleet Street, afterwards No. 53, having succeeded P. Overton (1710-1745), who succeeded John Senex (1695-1710), who is believed to have acquired the business and stock of charts of John Seller, the famous hydrographer of the Hermitage, Wapping, who flourished from about 1670 onwards. *Vide* Wilson (William), *History of the Three Ancient Firms of Chart-Publishers. London*, Imray, Laurie, Norie, and Wilson, Ltd,. 1917 (iv) + 15 pp. *Sm.* 4°.

[2] *Topographical Description*, p. vi.   [3] Jefferys died 20 November 1771.

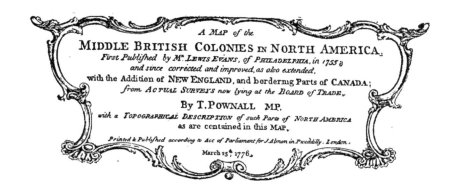

A MAP of the
MIDDLE BRITISH COLONIES IN NORTH AMERICA,
First Publifhed by Mr. LEWIS EVANS, of PHILADELPHIA, in 1755 ;
and since corrected and improved, as also extended,
with the Addition of NEW ENGLAND, and bordering Parts of CANADA;
from ACTUAL SURVEYS now lying at the Board of Trade,
By T. POWNALL M.P.
with a TOPOGRAPHICAL DESCRIPTION of such Parts of NORTH AMERICA
as are contained in this MAP,
Printed & Publifhed according to Act of Parliament for J. Almon in Picadilly. London,
March 25th 1776,

XII

1776. POWNALL'S RE-ISSUE OF EVANS' ORIGINAL PLATE OF 1755 IMPROVED, BUT WITHOUT THE EXTENSION

N 1776 Thomas Pownall re-issued Evans' original Map of 1755 (No. II) with a new title as shown above, and with numerous alterations engraved on the old plate to bring it up to date, as more particularly detailed in the next chapter.

The old plate not being sufficiently large to include the desired additions on the Eastern side, they were engraved on a separate copper-plate some 7 inches wide. The separate impressions from the two plates were afterwards pasted together to form one complete Map, and in order to join up properly, the right-hand border of the old Map was cut away or covered over, a new Eastern border having been re-engraved on the extension.

The copy here described is an impression from the old plate after the corrections had been made, but before the right-hand border had been cut away or pasted over. The Map was probably not actually published in this form, as, of course, without the extension, it does not include the additions mentioned in the title. The impression under notice may have been merely a proof, but as it is the only copy as yet seen by the writer without the wing joined on, it was thought worthy of inclusion.

31

The alterations made by Pownall on the old plate may be seen by comparison of the facsimiles of No. II and No. XIII accompanying this volume. In the latter the old plate (No. II) extended as far East as Newport, Rhode Island; the remainder being the extension made by Pownall in 1776. In the facsimile No. XIII the corrected old plate and the new extension are shown separately as (*a*) and (*b*).

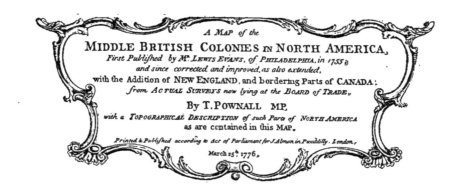

A MAP of the
MIDDLE BRITISH COLONIES IN NORTH AMERICA,
First Publifhed by Mr. LEWIS EVANS, of PHILADELPHIA, in 1755;
and since corrected and improved, as also extended,
with the Addition of NEW ENGLAND, and bordering Parts of CANADA:
from ACTUAL SURVEYS now lying at the BOARD of TRADE,
By T. POWNALL M.P.
with a TOPOGRAPHICAL DESCRIPTION of such Parts of NORTH AMERICA
as are contained in this MAP,
Printed & Publifhed according to Act of Parliament for J. Almon, in Piccadilly, London,
March 25th 1776,

XIII

1776. POWNALL'S RE-ISSUE OF EVANS' ORIGINAL PLATE IMPROVED, WITH THE EXTENSION

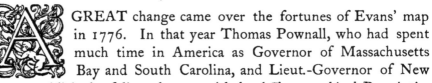

A GREAT change came over the fortunes of Evans' map in 1776. In that year Thomas Pownall, who had spent much time in America as Governor of Massachusetts Bay and South Carolina, and Lieut.-Governor of New Jersey, published a folio volume entitled, *A Topographical Description of such parts of North America as are contained in the* (annexed) *Map of the Middle British Colonies &c. in North America.*[1]

Pownall, after his return from America, continued to take the greatest interest in the welfare of the Colonies, as witness his famous work *The Administration of the Colonies,* which ran through several editions. The increasing public interest taken in the affairs of the Colonies at the outbreak of the Revolution, doubtless prompted the publication of the *Topographical Description.*

That work may be described as a new and much enlarged edition of both Evans' Map and his *Analysis* of 1755.

As to the Map, Pownall appears to have been in possession of the original Evans copper-plate (No. II) engraved by Jas. Turner in Philadelphia, and he uses it as the basis of his improved Map. The title is now completely altered, as may be seen from the facsimile

[1] London : J. Almon, 1776, vi. + 46 pp. + Appendix 16 pp. and map.

F

given at the head of this chapter, when compared with that of No. II. The old engraver's imprint *Engrav'd by Ja' Turner in Philadelphia*, still remains to the left of the cartouche, thus proving conclusively the use of the original copper-plate.

The alterations and additions in the Western half of the Map are not numerous, but are very important. Perhaps the most interesting is the insertion of a dotted line representing the route taken by Christopher Gist on his famous journey in 1750-1 from Col. Cresap's in Maryland down the Ohio River to near the Falls, and thence back to Roanoak River in North Carolina. Pownall (*in Topographical Description, Appendix No. VI*) prints Gist's Journal in full, which extends to ten large folio pages, and is intensely interesting when read-in with the Map by the lettered references in the margin, indicating the positions of the places mentioned and passed through.

But probably the most important addition is the alternative course of the River Ohio, as laid down by a double dotted line from Shawane T. to near the mouth of Kentucke River. A new legend engraved on the plate states "*The Peck'd Line is a supposed Course of the R^r Ohio "form'd so as to coincide wth C^t Gordon's Latitudes and Gist's courses.*" Pownall also prints (as *Appendix IV.* in *Top. Desc.*) long "*Extracts "from the Journal of Captain Harry Gordon, Chief Engineer in the "Western Department in North America, who was sent from Fort Pitt "on the River Ohio, down the said River, &c. to Illinois, in* 1766," which are of great interest when read-in with the Map by the lettered references.

The whole of the Map East of the longitude of Philadelphia is greatly changed, and is filled with new details. The old right-hand border, which in the original Evans plate was placed at about 4° east of Philadelphia, is cut off, or covered over, and the Map is now extended eastward to about 9°. The new portion of 5° appears to have been engraved on a separate plate, and, after separate printing, the impressions from each plate were neatly pasted together to form one map, as more fully explained in the previous chapter. In the ocean and in various other blank spaces, are Lists of the Counties and Townships of the various

Colonies, numbered to correspond with numbered references in the body of the Map.

The Map in its present altered and extended form is hardly to be recognized as being partly printed from Evans' old copper-plate corrected. But a comparison of the facsimile of the original (No. II) with that of the present issue, No. XIII (both of which accompany this volume), will make this fact apparent, and will also indicate the alterations and additions which have been made.

In the Preface to the *Topographical Description*, Pownall first reprints Evans' Preface to the *Analysis* of 1755, and then goes on to describe the additions and corrections he has made to the Map, and the sources from whence he derived his information. Speaking of Evans' original Map he says:

" The Western Division of this present map was composed and published
" at the Commencement of the late War in America. It was found by the
" Officers and Servants of the Crown to have that Degree of Precision, that it
" was used by them both in England and in America, and served every practical
" Purpose during the War. Those who have served and travelled in America,
" have had few Occasions of correcting it; on the contrary, its Exactness as far
" as a general Map means to go, as far as a Map on this small Scale could go,
" has generally been confirmed by Experience on the Spot. In any Transactions
" since the War, where local Precision has been necessary, this Map has been
" referred to, not simply in private but public Transactions, such as the great
" Indian Purchase and Cession. The Boundaries by which the Propositions
" for the Purchase of Lands on the Ohio were made to the Boards of Trade
" and Treasury, were marked and settled on this Map. When the Servants of
" the Crown proposed in the House of Commons the Clause for the Limits of
" the Government of Quebec; and when the Line of those Limits was there
" opposed, both Sides, with this Map in their Hands, argued from it."

After describing the alterations and corrections he has made to Evans' original Map in Virginia, Maryland, Pennsylvania, New Jersey, and New York, and quoting his authorities for the same, Pownall goes on to mention the additions he has made in the New England portion:

" What there was wanting to a compleat Map of New England, is now
" added from later Information, and from later Draughts and Surveys deposited
" at the Board of Trade, which the Earl of Dartmouth permitted me to have
" copied for the Benefit of the Public. These new Parts which I have added
" are plotted down in the Form in which I think every Map which can offer

"to give the Face of the Country should be drawn, tracing the Features of it,
"and not in Default of that, filling up the Map with Writing. Instead of
"Writing I have put *Figures of Reference*, and the Writing is put in the
"Margin and in other blank Places."

Pownall then proceeds to make some curious comparisons, retro-
spective and prospective, which appear to be of sufficient interest to
repeat. He says:

"Many Tracts which the Geographer will see marked on Evans's Map,
"in the Western Parts, and which were, when it was first published, mere
"Indian or Traders Paths through the Wilderness, are now in Course of a
"very few years become great Waggon Roads. Many Indian Settlements
"being merely a *Collection of Wigwams* or Cabins, must now be marked as
"County Towns. Many other particulars marked in the Map, and noticed in
"the original Analysis, which were, 20 Years ago, Matter of practical Informa-
"tion, and useful to the Service, ceasing, perhaps, now to have that Use, may
"yet be amusing as *Matters of curious Antiquity*, become so at this early Period.
"It will be curious in a few Years, as the Face of the Country changes and is
"totally altered, to view in this Map, and to read in this Description; what
"it was in its natural State, and how the Settlements began to expand, and
"had extended themselves in 20 Years."

How prophetic and yet how true! Oh shade of Pownall! what
wouldst thou now say couldst thou but see the changes which seven
score more years and four, have wrought o'er the spirit of thy
dream!

Pownall concludes his long and interesting Preface with some very
caustic remarks on the pirated copy of Evans' Map published by the
late Thomas Jefferys in 1758 (*vide* No. IV), but it is curious to note
that he makes no mention of the original pirated issue by Kitchin in
1756 (*vide* No. III), nor of the later and distinct one by Bowles (*vide*
No. V). As these remarks of Pownall were the direct incentive to the
present bibliographical investigation, it may be as well to repeat them
in full.

"A pirated Copy of this Map, soon after it came to England, was in a
"most audacious Manner published by the late Thomas Jefferys, under a
"false Pretence of Improvements, Lewis Evans's Name was put to it; and
"this Plagiarism was falsely sold as Evans's Map improved; by which that
"very laborious and ingenious, but poor Man, was deprived of the Benefit
"of his Work. The Engraver was so totally ignorant of the Principles on
"which the Original was formed, that although he traced the Lines of the

"Rivers and Roads in the usual Way, yet it can scarce be called a Copy.
"The Mountains in America, which give the real Features to the Face of it,
"run in Ridges of a specific Direction, do in Places here and there run up
"into Peaks; do in others end abruptly in Knobs and Bluff-points; do inter-
"lock and have Gaps; all which Particulars were in the Original with a
"scrupulous Attention plotted and set down; as also the Parts where these
"Ridges spread into hilly Land. The Officer or the Geographer will look in
"vain for this Precision in the pirated Copy. The blundering Copyist thought,
"that the filling the Places where he happened to meet with the Word
"*Mountains*, with the Engraver's common Marks scratched in at random, was
"doing the Business, by which he has put Mountains where they are not; and
"has converted great Swamps into Mountains; and in other parts has totally
"omitted the Marks of high Ground, because he did not understand those
"Marks which were used to express such high Ground, without presuming to
"give the Range and Form, where that was not yet known. So far as respects
"the Face of the Country, this Thing of Jefferys might as well be a Map of
"the Face of the Moon. Further, in the Original there was observed a
"scrupulous Caution not to deceive; the Parts which were drawn from Report
"and Computation, and collected from Journals, are in the Original engraved
"in a slighter Manner, and very differently from those Parts which are laid
"down from actual Surveys; neither the Eye, the Ideas, nor the Spirit of the
"Copyist went to the Marking this; and all Parts stand equal in authority in
"his false [1] Copy.

"'The Plate of this blundering Copy has, in the Course of Trade, by
"Purchase, fallen into the Hands of Mr. Sayer of Fleet-street, a Man of
"Reputation in a very extensive Line of Business. He very honourably told
"me, that if the Plate stood as a single Article in his Shop, he would destroy
"it directly; but that it made Part of an Atlas already published by him; [2]
"and was also part of another [3] very soon to be published by him, which cost
"many thousand Pounds; and that he did not know how to take it out of
"these Collections. I can only say, it will disgrace any Collection in which it
"stands, and that I am sorry it is to disgrace any coming from a Shop in
"which there are so many valuable Maps and Charts. Neither this improved
"Map nor the following Sheets are published with any View of Profit to the
"Editor; if any should accrue it will be given to Mr Evans's Daughter or her
"Children."

Pownall's accusation of piracy against Jefferys, and his protest
against the continued use of the plate by Sayer were not confined to
the preface of the *Topographical Description*. In the British Museum,

---

[1] Reads *pirated* in the prospectus. *Vide* next page.
[2] *A General Topography of North America.* London: R. Sayer and T. Jefferys, 1768.
[3] (?) *American Atlas.* London: R. Sayer and J. Bennett, 1775, or possibly he is referring to the then forthcoming new edition of the American Atlas afterwards published in 1776.

(11900, c. 5) there is fortunately preserved a copy of the original prospectus issued by J. Almon, announcing that,

> "speedily will be published A map of the Middle British Colonies in North
> "America. First published by Mr. Lewis Evans, of Philadelphia, in 1755;
> "and since corrected and improved, as also extended, with the Addition of
> "New England, &c., and bordering Parts of Canada; from actual Surveys
> "now lying at the Board of Trade. By T. Pownall, M.P., Late Governor,
> "&c., &c. With a Topographical Description of such Parts of North America
> "as are contained in the Map."

The above heading is followed by *Extract from the Preface*. The part relating to Jefferys is slightly different in the wording to what actually afterwards appeared in the published work, but is, if anything, more forcible. For instance, the first sentence reads: "This "map, soon after it came to England, was, in a most audacious "manner, pirated by the late Thomas Jefferys, under a false pretence "of improvements." The part relating to Sayer is identical in both prospectus and book.

These forcible remarks, so widely published, evidently had some effect on Mr. Sayer, for in the 1776 edition of the *American Atlas* the offending plate (which had appeared in the 1775 edition of that work, *vide* No. XI) was withdrawn, and a Map of Lake Champlain substituted for it in the Table of Contents.

According to the *Dictionary of National Biography*, xlvi, 267, Pownall "in 1785, had prepared a second edition (*i.e.* of the *Topo-* "*graphical Description*) with very many additions, which was probably "identical with the copy sold at New York about 1856 (Drake, "*History of Boston*, 1857, p. 655[1]). He also meditated publishing a "French translation for the benefit of the daughter of Evans (Franklin, "*Works*, x, 198-201)."

Neither the second edition in English nor the French translation appear ever to have been published, but it is quite clear Pownall had them both in contemplation, for in a letter he wrote from Lausanne,

---

[1] Drake says: "A copy of it [i.e., *Topographical Description and Map*], with MS. "additions by Gov. Pownall himself, was recently imported by Mr. Welford, of New "York, and sold at auction. Its present fortunate possessor is unknown to me."

3rd July 1785, to his friend Franklin at Passy, just before the latter's return to America, he says:

> "I received at Marseilles your letter by Mr Partridge, respecting the "nature of the account made out by the editor and bookseller of my map and "description of the States of America. I had already done in the matter every "thing in my power when I was on the spot, and pressed the point stronger "than I should have done, had it been for my account; but, when I con-"sidered it, as what I really wished, the doing an act of charity to the daughter "of an ingenious and ill-treated man, I exerted more pains about it than is "my ordinary custom. I wished to make my intended charity as efficient and "productive as possible. If I were on the spot I could not do more. I have "prepared a second edition, with very many additions. If you will recommend "to me any person who will translate it into French, I will publish this edition "in France and give the whole profits to Evans's daughter." [1]

Evans' daughter seems to have been a favourite with both Franklin and Pownall. In fact Franklin's wife was her godmother, as appears from a letter written by Franklin to his wife, dated London 22 July 1774: [2]

> "I enclose a letter I have just received from your goddaughter, Mrs Barry. "I wrote to you before, that she had married the captain of a ship in the "Levant trade. She is now again at Tunis, where you will see she has lately "lain in of her third child. Her father, you know, was a geographer, and his "daughter has some connexion, I think, with the whole globe; being born "herself in America, and having her first child in Asia, her second in Europe, "and now her third in Africa."

---

[1] Sparks' *Franklin*, x, 198.   [2] *Ibid.* viii, 125.

ARMS OF THOMAS POWNALL
From the Dedication on the Original
Map of 1755

A GENERAL MAP OF THE
MIDDLE BRITISH COLONIES,
IN AMERICA.
containing VIRGINIA, MARYLAND, THE DELAWARE COUNTIES,
PENNSYLVANIA AND NEW JERSEY.
With the addition of NEW YORK, and of the Greatest Part of NEW ENGLAND,
as also of the Bordering Parts of THE PROVINCE OF QUEBEC,
improved from several Surveys made after the late War.
By Officers in his
Majesty's Service.

XIV

1776. SAYER AND BENNETT'S FIRST RE-ISSUE OF THE SAYER AND JEFFERYS PLATE OF 1775 IMPROVED

THE old Kitchin-Jefferys-Sayer and Jefferys copper-plate which had already done duty for twenty years (*vide* Nos. III, IV, VI, X, and XI), although withdrawn in disgrace from the *American Atlas* of 1776 after Pownall's emphatic protests, was by no means yet done with, for it now took on a new lease of life, and had more than thirty years yet to live, as we shall see.

On the 15th of October in the same year it re-appeared in a new guise, yet so strangely altered as to be almost unrecognizable, but it is our old friend all the same.

There seems to be no end to the variations of this plate, for it has recently come to the notice of the writer that there are even two issues in its present shape, both bearing the date 15 Octr 1776. Both are found as separate maps, and either one or the other was included as Map No. IV in *The American Military Pocket Atlas*, published by R. Sayer and J. Bennet in 1776, the first state in early copies of that work, and the second in later issues.

The title of the Atlas bears no date, but the Dedication to Governor Pownall is dated 1776. In this Dedication the Editors say:

"SIR,

"As we undertook this Work for the use of the Military Gentlemen at
"your recommendation, we cannot but hope that the avowed patronage of a
"person so well informed in Geography, and having such a particular know-
"ledge of the country of North America, may recommend it to the public; we
"therefore presume to dedicate it to You. To You we owe our just acknow-
"ledgements for having enabled us to rectify former mistakes, to offer details
"hitherto unknown, and to collect a very great variety of interesting objects,
"within a moderate compass. Notwithstanding our utmost assiduity and
"attention to compleat your idea; we have still reason to wish this work could
"have been rendered more worthy of your patronage and acceptance, and that
"it might shew in a manner adequate to our wishes, the respect and gratitude
"with which we have the honour to be,
"Sir, Your most humble and devoted Servants,
"THE EDITORS.
"*Fleet Street*, 1776."

In the Advertisement which follows the Dedication, the Editors, speaking of the Map of the Middle Colonies, says that it has "been "collated with and corrected by Governor Pownall's late Map." From the Dedication it is quite clear that Pownall authorized and approved the re-issue of the Evans' Map in this corrected form, but one is at a loss to surmise why he allowed Evans' name to be altogether omitted from it, after all he had written in his *Topographical Description* only a few months before about the previous injustice to Evans.

As compared with the previous issue of this plate in 1775 (No. XI), in its present altered form, nine and a half inches of the outside top border line have been cut away in the centre, and in the resulting space a new headline title, "The Seat of War in the Middle "British Colonies, containing Virginia, Maryland, The Delaware "Counties, &ca." has been engraved.

The ornamental cartouche is entirely re-engraved in a different design, and the main title is also entirely re-engraved, and the wording of it greatly altered, as may be seen from the facsimile at the head of this chapter. The imprint is in one line in very small letters in the lower right-hand corner. "*London. Printed for R. Sayer & J. Bennett*, "*Map, Chart & Printsellers, No. 53 Fleet Street, as the Act directs*,

G

" 15ᵗʰ Oĉʳ 1776." Beneath the imprint is the scale of 130 miles, which in the former issues was in the top left-hand corner.

Although Evans' name is now omitted from the title, the main delineations of the country in the central part of the Map conform to his original. In faĉt that part of the old Kitchin-Jefferys-Sayer and Jefferys plate has now been specially correĉted to accord with Evans' original in those particulars to which Pownall so strongly takes exception when protesting against the Jefferys piracy in his *Topographical Description* already quoted. The spurious mountains are eliminated and the swamps reinstated. But in the Northern and Western regions the Map is hardly recognizable. All the legends relating to the Indians, engraved in various parts of the Map in all the previous editions, are now omitted, as are also the several Tables of Distances, formerly placed in the blanks in the Atlantic Ocean. The course of the Ohio River is greatly altered West of 8° from Philadelphia, and now conforms more nearly to the alternative " peck'd line " as laid down by Pownall in his Map of 1776 (*vide* No. XIII, page 34), as showing the supposed course of the River according to the Journals of Gist and Gordon.

The shapes of Lakes Erie and Ontario are considerably changed, and the country to the north of them is filled in and lettered. Lake Huron begins to take definite shape. The little inset Map, " A sketch of the remaining Part of Ohio R., &c.," which had appeared in all previous editions is now much enlarged, and is carried right up to the top border in place of the Dedication in Evans' original, or in place of the scale and two paragraphs of text in the reprints. It is now entitled, " A Sketch of the Upper Parts of Canada," and includes the whole of Lake Superior and some country to the north of it. The whole of the Country to the North-West of the Ohio River, the Lakes Erie and Ontario, and the River St. Lawrence, is now marked *PROVINCE* OF *QUEBEC* in a large lettering extending for some 26 inches in a diagonal curve right across the Map from between 38° and 39° at the left border to the head of Lake Champlain. To the right of the title cartouche is another large lettering, *CANADA*, 7½ inches long, placed half an inch below the top border. These alterations were presumably made to show the Boundaries of the Province of Quebec as defined by the Quebec Act of 1774.[1]

It now remains to describe the differences in the two issues of 1776. From the facsimile of the title of the first, as given at the head of this chapter, it will be observed by comparison with the facsimile of the second in the next chapter, that as yet no mention is made that the Map had been " corrected from Governor Pownall's late Map " 1776," but merely that it was " improved from several surveys made " after the late War by Officers in his Majesty's Service." In the body of the Map the following particulars will serve for identification of the first issue, though there are other minute differences not easily notice-able or describable in detail, *e.g.* in the second issue there are numerous additional mountains, rivers, and place-names in Virginia, south of James River.

(*a*) In the left lower corner the old 4-line legend relating to the Falls of the Ohio, placed between 37° and 38° to the West of the River, still remains.

(*b*) The Great Kanhawa River, south of its junction with Green Briar River, is lettered New River, and none of its tributaries are named.

(*c*) The lettering of Lake Ontario is in three lines, *LAKE ONTARIO/* or *CADARAQUI/* (*i.e.* the Fair Lake)./

The differences in the second issue corresponding to the above-mentioned three points, are detailed in the next chapter.

[1] *Cf.* p. 27, *ante.*

A GENERAL MAP OF THE
MIDDLE BRITISH COLONIES,
IN AMERICA,
containing VIRGINIA MARYLAND, THE DELAWARE COUNTIES,
PENNSYLVANIA AND NEW JERSEY.
With the addition of NEW YORK and of the Greatest Part of NEW ENGLAND
as also of the Bordering Parts of THE PROVINCE OF QUEBEC,
improved from several Surveys made after the late War.
and Corrected
from GOVERNOR POWNALLS Late Map 1776.

XV

1776. SAYER AND BENNETT'S SECOND RE-ISSUE OF THE PLATE OF 1775, IMPROVED AND CORRECTED FROM GOVERNOR POWNALL'S LATE MAP

HE general features of this second issue of 1776 are the same as in the foregoing. The headline-title, and the imprint are exactly the same, but the main title has been altered in the last two lines, so as to state that the Map is now "corrected from Governor Pownall's Late Map 1776." The differences in the last two lines will be observed by comparing the facsimile above with that of No. XIV.

The general description of the first issue being equally applicable to this second, need not be repeated. It merely remains to point out the differences corresponding to points *a, b,* and *c,* mentioned at the end of the previous chapter.

(*a*) The legend relating to the Falls of the Ohio has been deleted.

(*b*) The Great Kanawha River, south of its junction with Green Briar River, is lettered *Great Kanawha R.* (reading downwards) and *the New River* (reading upwards), and its tributaries are now named, *Blue Stone R., Walkers R.*

44

Peak Cr., Reedy Cr., on the Western side, and *Little R.*
and *Reeves Island Cr.* on the Eastern side.

(*c*) Lake Ontario is now lettered in one line, simply *LAKE
ONTARIO,* in large italic capitals along the centre.

As mentioned in the previous chapter there are other minute
alterations difficult to describe in detail, but the above three points are
amply sufficient for identification. The Map, in its present state, is
met with both separately, and as Map No. 4 in late issues of the
American Military Pocket Atlas. As that Atlas is not dated on the
title, it is reasonable to suppose that it remained current till the close
of the war. In 1794 the plate was again altered and re-issued as
"A New and general Map" (*vide* No. XVIII).

B O W L E S's
NEW POCKET MAP
OF THE
MIDDLE BRITISH COLONIES,
IN AMERICA, VIZ.
VIRGINIA, MARYLAND, DELAWARE, PENSYLVANIA,
NEW JERSEY, NEW YORK, CONNECTICUT & RHODE ISLAND.
Comprehending alſo the
HABITATIONS & HUNTING COUNTRIES OF THE
CONFEDERATE INDIANS;
by Lewis Evans.

Printed for the Proprietor CARINGTON BOWLES,
Nº 69 in Sᵗ Pauls Church Yard,
LONDON.

XVI

[*c.* 1780 ?]. CARINGTON BOWLES' RE-ISSUE OF HIS PLATE OF
1771[-4 ?]

UR old acquaintance, the Bowles Piracy of the Kitchin-Jefferys piracy, which had already done duty as Nos. V, VII, VIII, and IX, now comes to life again, rejuvenated and rehabilitated as "Bowles's New Pocket Map." As will be seen from the facsimile above, compared with No. IX, the ornamental cartouche and the title of 1771 have been removed, and an entirely new title, without any border, inserted in its place.

The date of this issue is somewhat uncertain, but the title *New Pocket Map*, indicates that it was a separate publication. It is also found as a sheet Map, No. 33, in an undated edition of *Bowles's Universal Atlas* [London: Printed for and sold by the Proprietor, Carington Bowles, &c. *folio*] from which fact certain deductions can be drawn. As some of the Maps in that Atlas are dated as late as 1780, it is clear this issue of Evans's Map was at least current in that year, although it is quite possible it may have been actually published

46

previously in its separate form as a *New Pocket Map.* On the other hand, as the title still speaks of the *Middle British Colonies,* it must have been published before the Peace of 1782-3. So in assigning the date, *c.* 1780, to this issue, we cannot in any case be very far wrong.

As compared with the 1774 (?) Edition (No. IX), besides the alteration in the title, the following differences are noticeable.

> (*a*) The Eastern shore of Lake Huron has been extended North from about 43° 50′ to 45° 10′, and the Western shore to about 44° 10′, at which point it joins the border of the inset. New rivers and lakes have been inserted in the District to the North of Lake Ontario, and the following new names appear on the Lake shore between Ft. Toronto and Kente, viz., Tegaogan and Ganaraske, while the small lake above the latter, on the line of 3° W. Long., is now marked L. Quentio. These insertions, which would have overrun the old ornamental title-cartouche of No. IX, were probably the cause of the deletion of the border and the re-engraving of the title in narrower form.
>
> (*b*) The long legend to the North of Lake Erie, relating to the Confederates, has been entirely deleted, and the resulting space filled in with Rivers, Trees, and Mountains.

Doubtless there are other differences, but if so they are unimportant and so minute as not to be readily detected.

Although this Map cannot compare for accuracy and up-to-dateness with Sayer and Bennett's editions of 1776, the publishers deserve some credit for retaining the name of Evans as the author. But the old physical errors in the mountains and swamps, to which Pownall in 1776 took such strong exception when describing the Jefferys piracy, still remain, for the Bowles' plate, as has been shown, was in itself, after all, but a piracy from the Kitchin-Jefferys piracy (*vide* No. V).

BOWLES's
NEW POCKET MAP
OF THE FOLLOWING
INDEPENDENT STATES OF
NORTH AMERICA, VIZ.
VIRGINIA, MARYLAND, DELAWARE, PENSYLVANIA,
NEW JERSEY, NEW YORK, CONNECTICUT & RHODE ISLAND.
Comprehending alſo the
HABITATIONS & HUNTING COUNTRIES OF THE
CONFEDERATE INDIANS;
by Lewis Evans.

Printed for the Proprietor CARINGTON BOWLES,
Nº 69 in S.ᵗPauls Church Yard,
LONDON.

XVII
[1784]. CARINGTON BOWLES' RE-ISSUE OF No. XVI

COMPARISON of the title, as given above, with No. XVI, shows that this issue no longer represents the *Middle British Colonies*, but the *Independent States of North America*, and hence could not have been published till after the Peace of 1783. The title, *New Pocket Map*, makes it clear that it was still intended to be issued in separate form, but it also appears with the same title as a sheet Map, No. 34, in *Bowles's Universal Atlas*, a later undated edition than the one referred to in the previous chapter.

This re-issue of the Atlas was doubtless made shortly after the Peace, for the Map of North America, No. 31, which in the former edition was undated, has now been brought up to date so as to show the United States, and bears the imprint, *Published as the Act directs 12 April* 1784. An entirely new Map, No. 32, *Bowles's New Pocket Map of the United States of America*, bearing the same imprint,

48

12 *April* 1784, has been inserted, consequently all the remaining Maps in the Atlas are advanced one in numeration, so that the present edition of Evans becomes No. 34 instead of No. 33. Although no date has been inserted on it, it is fairly obvious, from its new title, that it was revised at the same time, and as there are no Maps dated later than 1784 in this edition of the *Universal Atlas*, the date [1784] may confidently be assigned.

Evans' Map in its present state is also found without alteration in later issues of the *Universal Atlas*, as published by Carington Bowles, down to the time of his death, 20 June 1793. From this fact reasons were given in the First Edition of this Essay for assigning the date of this issue as [1792-3?], because the copy described was found in an edition of *Bowles's Univeral Atlas*, in which some of the Maps were dated as late as 1792. Finding Evans' Map in company with others dated 1792, and observing that it showed the lettering *Vermont*, presumably intended to indicate the State admitted to the Union in 1791, the writer argued that the Map could not have been issued before 1791, or after 1793, when Bowles died. But the 1784 edition of the *Universal Atlas* had not then been identified. As it is now found that the Maps of North America and the United States, actually dated 1784, both show *Vermont*, it is clear that that lettering on them and also on Evans' Map, was not intended to indicate the State as admitted to the Union in 1791, but the old independent State of Vermont as so declared by its inhabitants in January 1777.

It may therefore be fairly concluded that the present state of our Map was first published in 1784, and remained current till the death of Carington Bowles in 1793, after which it was again revised and re-issued by Bowles and Carver as described in Chapter XIX.

Comparing the present issue of the *New Pocket Map* with Carington Bowles's previous one (No. XVI) the principal alterations are as follows:

 (*a*) The lettering *VERMONT* is added, but no new place names or additional features have been inserted. The lettering " Part of | New Hampshire," which in the previous edition was all in one line, part on each side of Connecticut River, is now in two lines, both on the East side.

(*b*) The three Legends relating to the Indians have been deleted, *i.e.*, the one in six lines immediately above the inset, the one below the inset, and the one in the lower left corner. The legend relating to the Ohio Lands, on the right-hand side of the Map between 39° and 41°, has also been removed, but the old lettering, *OHIO*, which was marked both North and South of the River in all the previous Bowles' editions (Nos. V, VII, VIII, IX, and XVI) still remains (*cf.* No. XIX).

(*c*) The "Boundary of the United States" (so lettered in Lake Ontario) is shown by a bold dotted line through Lakes Ontario, Erie, and Huron.

(*d*) Only the scale and the upper Legend relating to portages and the navigation of Rivers, remain in the top left-hand corner above the inset sketch Map of Ohio River.

The old long lettering *CANADA* still remains, starting in the Ohio district, where it is now, of course, out of place as far as the country to the South of Lake Erie is concerned.

The old physical errors in the mountains and swamps, to which Pownall in 1776 took such strong exception in describing the Jefferys piracy, still remain uncorrected.

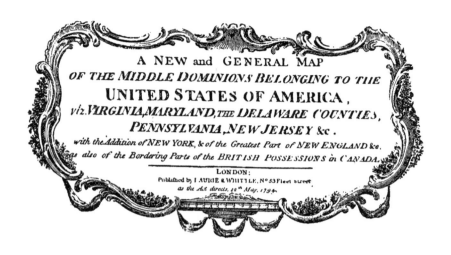

XVIII

1794-1814. Laurie and Whittle's Re-issue of Sayer and Bennett's Plate of 1776

 N 1794 our other old friend, the Kitchin-Jefferys-Sayer and Jefferys-Sayer and Bennett plate (Nos. III, IV, VI, X, XI, XIV, and XV), last used in 1776, again comes to life as " A New and General Map " after some eighteen years' slumber (unless used in the meantime in some edition not yet identified). The name of Evans had already been omitted from the title of 1776, and now in 1794 Pownall is also relegated to oblivion, although but few alterations have been made in the general details of the Map since his corrections of 1776.

The new title, as may be seen from the facsimile above, is entirely different from that of No. XV, although the ornamental border is the same.

In the present edition a dotted line has been run from the River St. Lawrence through Lakes Ontario, Erie, and part of Huron, to show the boundary between the United States and Canada. The dotted boundary line is also shown in the inset through the upper part of Lake Huron and through Lake Superior to the St. Louis River. The title of the inset, which in the 1776 edition read " *A Sketch of the*

Upper Parts of Canada," has now been altered to "*A Sketch of the Upper Parts to shew the Remainder of the Lakes*," but nothing in the Lake Region has been added except the Boundary Line.

The lettering *State of Vermont* has been inserted, but without the addition of any new names or features. A new large lettering *KENTUCKY*, presumably intended to show the position of the new State admitted to the Union in 1792, has been added in the country immediately to the *North* of the Ohio River, whereas of course its proper position should have been on the *South* side of the River. The same error occurs in placing the name in the inset.

The headline title " The Seat of War " etc., which appeared in the 1776 edition, is, of course, omitted, and the border line reinstated. The old lettering in the South-East corner *Atlantic Ocean*, is now added to, so as to read *Western or Atlantic Ocean*. The old long lettering *PROVINCE OF QUEBEC* still remains, the first two words of which should, of course, have been deleted, as the word *Province* is placed in the country to the South-West of Lake Erie, which passed to the United States at the Peace of 1783, and was no longer known as part of Quebec. From the imprint it seems probable that this Map was sold separately in 1794, but it also appears in *A New Universal Atlas* published by Robert Laurie and James Whittle in 1796, and as Sheet No. 71 in their *Third Edition* of that work issued in 1799. It is also to be found as Sheet No. 47 in *A new and elegant Imperial Sheet Atlas* published by the same firm in 1798, and again as Sheet 50 in their *New Editions* of 1807 and 1808. In all these Atlases the plate still bears the date of 12th May 1794, though, as the paper varies, apparently reprinted for each edition. It is quite possible the map may have been included in intermediate and later editions of these Atlases, for the firm of Laurie and Whittle carried on business till 1812.

At that date James Whittle took into partnership Richard Holmes Laurie, the son of Robert Laurie (presumably deceased), and the name of the firm then became inverted to J. Whittle and R. H. Laurie, under which style and title it was carried on till the death of James

Whittle in 1818. R. H. Laurie continued the business alone under his own name till his death in 1858, when he was succeeded by Alexander George Findlay, who conducted it till 1875, and who in his turn was succeeded by his nephews D. W., H. A., and W. R. Kettle. In 1903 the business became merged in the present well-known firm of Imray, Laurie, Norie and Wilson, Ltd., whose record at the present time can be traced back from the time of old John Seller (*c.* 1670) over a continuous trading period of 250 years!!![1]

Reverting to the particular map under notice, Mr. P. Lee Phillips in his *List of Atlases*,[2] 1909, vol. i, No. 720, quotes a *New Edition* of the *New and elegant Imperial Sheet Atlas* published by J. Whittle and R. H. Laurie 1813—[1814], which appears to contain the map of 1794 as Sheet No. 50. But whether or not any alterations in the imprint or in the map itself have been made at this late date, the writer is unable to say, as he has not met with this particular edition of the Atlas. Presuming the plate to be the same, even if altered, its currency has thus been traced for a continuous period of fifty-seven years, *i.e.*, from the time when Kitchin first issued it in 1756!

---

[1] The writer is indebted to his friend Mr. William Wilson for some of these particulars. *Vide op. cit.*, footnote, p. 30.

[2] Phillips (P. Lee), *A List of Geographical Atlases in the Library of Congress.* Washington, 1909-14, 3 vols. large 8vo.

BOWLE S's
NEW ONE - SHEET MAP
OF THE
INDEPENDENT STATES
——— OF ———

VIRGINIA, MARYLAND, DELAWARE, PENSYLVANIA·
NEW JERSEY, NEW YORK, CONNECTICUT, RHODE ISLAND &c.
Comprehending alfo the
HABITATIONS & HUNTING COUNTRIES OF THE
CONFEDERATE INDIANS;
by Lewis Evans,

Printed for the Proprietors BOWLES & CARVER,
Nº 69 in S.t Pauls Church Yard,
LONDON.

XIX

[1796-1800?] BOWLES AND CARVER'S RE-ISSUE OF CARINGTON
BOWLES' PLATE No. XVII

AFTER the death of Carington Bowles, 20 June 1793, his
son Henry Carington Bowles[1] carried on the business
with a Mr. Carver under the partnership style of Bowles
and Carver. They continued to publish the *Universal
Atlas* with their new imprint, but still undated. The old Bowles Plate
of Evans' Map again appears therein, this time as No. 33, and with
the title altered as shown in the headpiece above (Cf. No. XVII).

Considerable alterations have again been made in the plate. The
old name *Aquanishuonigy* is omitted, and the diftrict south of Lake
Erie and north of the Ohio River is now named *Western Territory*,
with a similar new lettering on the inset. The new State of Kentucky
(admitted 1792) is also marked in its proper position south of the
Ohio River; whereas in Laurie and Whittle's contemporary and rival

---

[1] Born 31 August 1763, died 1830. *Vide also* footnote, p. 24.

plate (No. XVIII) it was erroneously shown on the North of the River. Tennessee is also marked, but whether intended as the Territory (1794) or the State (1796), there is nothing to show.

A small district, corresponding somewhat to the present State of West Virginia, is marked " Indiana," but does not seem to have any connection with the position of Indiana Territory as organized in 1800, or the State as admitted in 1816, because it is south of the River Ohio in the angle made by the Little Kanhawa River. This Indiana seems to correspond almost exactly to the district marked by that name in Hutchins' *New Map of the Western Parts of Virginia*, etc., published by him in 1778. In his *Topographical Description of Virginia*, etc., published in the same year to accompany the Map, he says: " Indiana, as may be seen in my Map, lies within the territory " here described. It contains about three millions and an half of Acres, " and was granted to Samuel Wharton, William Trent, and George " Morgan, Esquires, and a few other persons, in the year 1768."

The old lettering *OHIO*, which was marked both North and South of the River in all the previous Bowles Editions (Nos. V, VII, VIII, IX, XVI, and XVII), has now been deleted. The old long lettering *CANADA* (cf. No. XVII), has at last been corrected. The first three letters *CAN* have been removed from the Ohio River District (now marked Western Territory), and re-engraved in the country to the North of Lake Erie, reading on with the three last letters *ADA*, the position of which has not been changed. The Western boundary of Pennsylvania is now shown by a dotted line, and some other dotted boundary lines in the same district have also been added. Doubtless there are other additions of minor importance, but the above will serve for identification.

The date of this edition is somewhat uncertain, but approximately it may be placed between 1796 (that is to say after the admission of Tennessee) and 1800 (see below). In all probability the map continued current in the *Universal Atlas* for many years later, as the firm of Bowles and Carver was carried on till 1832. In the *Universal Atlas* as issued by Bowles and Carver, all the imprints of the maps in Carington Bowles' edition are altered to that of the new firm, and all the dates are omitted, hence it is very difficult to assign an exact date. Turning to Map No. 31 in the same volume, in the *General Map of the United States* we find Louisiana and East and West Florida are specially designated as belonging to Spain. As Louisiana was retroceded to France in 1800 it may safely be assumed that this edition of the *Universal Atlas* (and consequently the map under notice contained in it) must have been issued before the date of that important event.

CONCLUSION

THE bibliographical and cartographical history of Evans' maps of 1749 and 1755 has now been traced from 1749 to about 1814 in no less than nineteen distinct and separate plates, viz.:

1 original Evans plate of 1749. No. I.
3 issues of the original Evans plate of 1755. Nos. II, XII, and XIII.
8 issues of the Kitchin pirated plate. Nos. III, IV, VI, X, XI, XIV, XV, and XVIII.
7 issues of the Bowles pirated plate. Nos. V, VII, VIII, IX, XVI, XVII, and XIX.

It is quite possible, indeed highly probable that other states, reprints or variations, still which have not as yet come under notice and the writer would be greatly obliged to any one who will call his attention to any issues not recorded in this Essay.

Enough has been written to show the extraordinary number of emanations from Evans' map of 1755, and the prominent place they took in the cartography of North America during the latter half of the eighteenth century and later. Quite apart from these actual copies, it would be interesting to trace and record the evident influence which they have exercised on the numerous maps of other cartographers who make no mention of Evans as their prototype. But the study of comparative cartography, although intensely interesting, can only be attempted in these strenuous times by a man of leisure who is fortunate enough to be able to devote the necessary time to it.

Considerable light has been shed in this little Essay on the tricks of trade of the map publishers, and the plagiarisms of the cartographers in Carington Bowles' edition are altered to that of the new firm, and all the dates are omitted, hence it is very difficult to assign an exact date. Turning to Map No. 31 in the same volume, in the *General Map of the United States* we find Louisiana and East and West Florida are specially designated as belonging to Spain. As Louisiana was retro-ceded to France in 1800 it may safely be assumed that this edition of the *Universal Atlas* (and consequently the map under notice con-tained in it) must have been issued before the date of that important event.

CONCLUSION

THE bibliographical and cartographical history of Evans' maps of 1749 and 1755 has now been traced from 1749 to about 1814 in no less than nineteen distinct and separate plates, viz.:

1 original Evans plate of 1749. No. I.

3 issues of the original Evans plate of 1755. Nos. II, XII, and XIII.

8 issues of the Kitchin piratical plate. Nos. III, IV, VI, X, XI, XIV, XV, and XVIII.

7 issues of the Bowles' piratical plate. Nos. V, VII, VIII, IX, XVI, XVII, and XIX.

It is quite possible, indeed highly probable, that other states, reprints or variations, exist which have not as yet come under notice, and the writer would be greatly obliged to any one who will call his attention to any issues not recorded in this Essay.

Enough has been written to show the extraordinary number of emanations from Evans' map of 1755, and the prominent place they took in the cartography of North America during the latter half of the eighteenth century and later. Quite apart from these actual copies, it would be interesting to trace and record the evident influence which they have exercised on the numerous maps of other cartographers who make no mention of Evans as their prototype. But the study of comparative cartography, although intensely interesting, can only be attempted in these strenuous times by a man of leisure who is fortunate enough to be able to devote the necessary time to it.

Considerable light has been shed in this little Essay on the tricks of trade of the map publishers, and the plagiarisms of the cartographers of the period. When it is realized that the same old copper-plate of the first London edition of Evans' map, engraved by Kitchin in 1756, was reissued as late as 1814 (*vide* No. XVIII) as *A New aud General Map* after a life of fifty-eight years, with numerous intermediate aliases, one is tempted to exclaim, " Good Evans is it possible! " Verily as the Preacher of old hath it, " there is no new thing under the sun."

of the period. When it is realized that the same old copper-plate of the first London edition of Evans' map, engraved by Kitchin in 1756, was reissued as late as 1814 (*vide* No. XVIII) as *A New aud General Map* after a life of fifty-eight years, with numerous intermediate aliases, one is tempted to exclaim, " Good Evans is it possible! " Verily as the Preacher of old hath it, " there is no new thing under the sun."

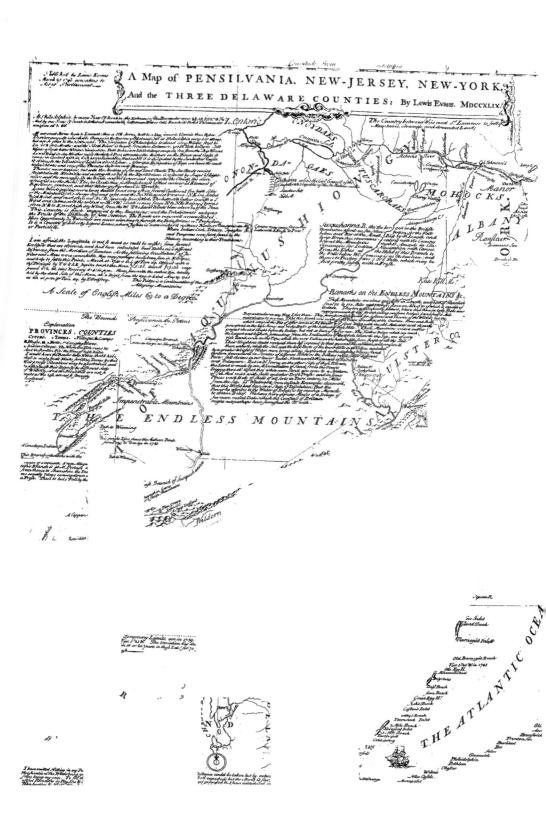

A Map of PENSILVANIA, NEW-JERSEY, NEW-YORK, And the THREE DELAWARE COUNTIES: By Lewis Evans. MDCCXLIX.